Digital

MARKETING SUCCESS

Your Digital Presence

John Monyjok Maluth

Copyright © 2024 John Monyjok Maluth

***

ISBN: 9798322578246
Discipleship Press
Web: www.discipleshippress.wordpress.com
Email: maluthabiel@gmail.com

~~***~~

+254 110 424 822
+211 927 145 394

P.O. Box 28448-00100, Nairobi Kenya

Library of Congress Control Number:

All rights reserved. No part of this book may be reproduced, stored in a retrieval system, or transmitted in any or by any means – electronic, mechanical, photocopying, recording, or otherwise- without prior permission in writing from the copyright holder.

DISCLAIMER:

This is a work of fiction. While inspired by real-world events, places, or concepts, the story and characters are entirely fictional. Any resemblance to actual persons, living or dead, or actual events is unintentional.

CONTENTS

CHAPTER 1: PANYIM'S DESIGN STUDIO 1
   What I Want You to Learn From My Studio 5
   Lesson 1: Your Work Must Be Clear Before Your Marketing Can Be Clear 6
   Lesson 2: Your Brand Story Is Not a Speech, It Is a Thread 7
   Lesson 3: The Internet Does Not Reward Perfection, It Rewards Presence 8
   Lesson 4: Your First Digital Asset Is Not a Website, It Is Your Identity 9
   Lesson 5: Your Digital Presence Has a Home Base 10
   Lesson 6: Your First Marketing Plan Should Fit Your Life, Not Your Fantasy
   11
   The Studio Audit: What You Should Do Today 12
   Back to the Story: Nyakor Walks In 14
   Chapter 1 Notes From Me to You 17
   Chapter 2: Panyim Expresses His Excitement 19
   Scene 1: The Waiting Room That Teaches You Everything 20
   Lesson 1: Turn Fear Into a Presentation You Can Repeat 21
   Scene 2: The Publish Button That Feels Like a Cliff 23
   Lesson 2: Excitement Is a Signal, Not a Plan 24
   Scene 3: Criticism Arrives, and You Learn What You Are Made Of 25
   Lesson 3: Your Response Strategy Is Part of Your Content Strategy 27
   Scene 4: The Creative Block That Comes After Success 28
   Lesson 4: Build a "Creative Recovery" Routine 29
   Scene 5: Visibility Does Not Happen Overnight, So You Must Become Patient
   on Purpose 30
   Lesson 5: Risk Is Required, but It Must Be Chosen 31
   Lesson 6: Use Self-Doubt as Fuel, Not as a Judge 31
   Putting It Into Digital Marketing Language 32
   Exercises: What I Want You to Do After This Chapter 33
   Closing: The Real Reward Is Who You Become 34

CHAPTER 3: THE CONCEPT OF DIGITAL PRESENCE 36
   What Digital Presence Really Means 37
   The Two Sides of Digital Presence: What You Control and What You Must
   Manage 38
   The First Trap: Comparison That Kills Authenticity 39
   Step 1: Identifying Your Passion 40
   Step 2: Creating Authentic Content 41
   Step 3: Choosing the Right Platforms 43
   Step 4: Creating a Content Calendar 44
   Step 5: Engaging With Your Audience 45
   Step 6: Measuring Success and Adapting 46
   The Digital Presence Stack: Home, Megaphone, and Story 47

  A Real Example: How I Would Build Digital Presence From Zero Today 48
  Common Mistakes I See and How I Fix Them 49
  Closing: Digital Presence Is Not a Mask, It Is a Mirror 49

CHAPTER 4: THE IMPORTANCE OF A WEBSITE 51

  A website is not a brochure, it is a home 51
  The website and the public square 52
  The biggest benefit: credibility you can control 53
  My turning point: I stopped building pages and started building paths 54
  What makes a website "strong" in digital marketing terms 55
  The essential pages I build first 56
  The website as a story machine 57
  The website as a conversion system 58
  Your website is where you build your list 59
  Search engines and the long game 60
  The website gives you a clean place to measure reality 61
  How I build a website when I want it to produce results 62
  A practical example from my world: turning "Kuel" into a website experience
  65
  Key lessons I want you to carry from this chapter 66

CHAPTER 5: DEVELOPING A CLEAR BRAND IDENTITY 68

  The night I learned that a brand is not a logo 68
  What "brand identity" really means 69
  Why brand identity matters more online than offline 70
  The three layers of brand identity I use 70
  Building your brand identity the way Nyakor made me do it 72
  Turning meaning into a message people can repeat 75
  Designing a visual identity that is usable, not just pretty 77
  The "identity test" I use before I publish anything 80
  Brand identity is also behavior 81
  A practical example: building Kuel's identity from the ground up 81
  Common mistakes that destroy brand identity 82
  Your Brand Kit (what to keep in one folder) 83
  A short studio exercise (do it today) 84
  Closing: the moment a brand becomes real 85

CHAPTER 6: SEARCH ENGINE OPTIMIZATION (SEO) 86

  1) What SEO really is (and what it is not) 86
  2) Start where most people skip: eligibility and trust 87
  3) How search works in simple human language 88
  4) Keywords are not "stuffing," they are listening 89
  5) The foundation: if your website is weak, SEO collapses 91
  6) On-page SEO: make each page speak clearly 92

7) CONTENT: THE BRIDGE BETWEEN YOU AND THE SEARCHER 94
8) TECHNICAL SEO: THE UNSEEN HERO 96
9) STRUCTURED DATA: HELP SEARCH ENGINES LABEL WHAT YOU BUILT 97
10) BACKLINKS: BUILDING BRIDGES, NOT BEGGING FOR VOTES 97
11) MEASUREMENT: SEO WITHOUT TRACKING IS JUST HOPE 98
12) PATIENCE: THE PART NOBODY WANTS, BUT EVERYBODY NEEDS 99
13) MY WEEKLY SEO RHYTHM (A SYSTEM YOU CAN REPEAT) 100
15) THE SEO PROMISE: YOUR WORK BECOMES DISCOVERABLE WHILE YOU SLEEP 101

CHAPTER 7: THE POWER OF SOCIAL MEDIA MARKETING 103

SOCIAL MEDIA IS NOT A BILLBOARD 103
CHOOSING PLATFORMS LIKE A STRATEGIST, NOT LIKE A TOURIST 104
YOUR FIRST JOB IS NOT POSTING, IT IS BECOMING RECOGNIZABLE 107
ENGAGEMENT IS A SKILL, NOT A PERSONALITY TRAIT 109
CONTENT STRATEGY: CONSISTENCY WITHOUT BURNOUT 110
COLLABORATION: BORROWED TRUST DONE THE RIGHT WAY 112
BUILDING A COMMUNITY, NOT JUST AN AUDIENCE 113
TURNING SOCIAL ATTENTION INTO BUSINESS RESULTS 114
METRICS THAT MATTER, WITHOUT BECOMING A SLAVE TO NUMBERS 116
HANDLING CRITICISM, LOW POSTS, AND THE "VOID" FEELING 117
STAYING CONSISTENT WHILE THE PLATFORMS CHANGE 119
THE FIRST POST THAT STARTS THE JOURNEY 119

CHAPTER 9: A COHESIVE DIGITAL MARKETING STRATEGY 121

THE PROBLEM MOST PEOPLE HAVE (AND WHY YOU MIGHT FEEL STUCK) 122
THE "SINGLE THREAD" RULE: ONE PROMISE, ONE AUDIENCE, ONE NEXT STEP 123
STEP 1: START WITH YOUR STORY, NOT YOUR TOOLS 124
STEP 2: BUILD YOUR "HOME BASE" (YOUR WEBSITE) AND GIVE EVERY PLATFORM A JOB
 125
STEP 3: CHOOSE PLATFORMS BASED ON YOUR PEOPLE, NOT YOUR EGO 126
STEP 4: CREATE A CONTENT CALENDAR THAT MATCHES YOUR REAL LIFE 127
STEP 5: MAKE ENGAGEMENT A STRATEGY, NOT A HABIT 128
STEP 6: BUILD MEASUREMENT INTO THE PLAN, SO YOU CAN ADAPT WITHOUT PANIC ... 130
STEP 7: KEEP CONSISTENCY, KEEP LEARNING, KEEP SHIPPING 131
PUTTING IT ALL TOGETHER: THE ONE-PAGE STRATEGY MAP I USE 131
A FULL EXAMPLE: HOW I WOULD APPLY THIS FOR A NEW DIGITAL BRAND 133
THE COMMON TRAPS THAT BREAK COHESION (AND HOW I AVOID THEM) 134
MY CLOSING LESSON FOR THIS CHAPTER 134

FINAL NOTE 136

COPIES, PERMISSIONS, AND BULK ORDERS 138

LEAVE A REVIEW 139

ABOUT THE AUTHOR 141

DISCLAIMER

This book uses a story to teach practical digital marketing. The characters, scenes, and dialogue are created for learning and illustration, even when they feel familiar. Any resemblance to real persons, living or dead, or real events is coincidental. The marketing principles, examples, and methods discussed are meant for education, and results will vary based on effort, budget, timing, and market conditions. Nothing in this book should be treated as legal, financial, or professional advice. You are responsible for how you apply the ideas, and you should seek qualified advice when you need it.

AUTHOR'S NOTE

I wrote this book as a bridge between craft and visibility. In the story, I am Panyim, a maker with a real product and real pride in where I come from, but with questions about how to be seen online. Nyakor enters as the marketer who can translate creativity into a digital presence that people can find, trust, and follow.

I chose a narrative approach because many people do not struggle with talent. They struggle with exposure, clarity, and consistency. A story lets me show fear, resistance, and breakthrough in a human way, while still giving you a working method you can copy. As you read, treat the scenes as a mirror: the emotions are there to keep you honest, and the lessons are there to keep you moving.

HOW TO USE THIS BOOK

Read it twice, in two different ways.

First pass: read like a story. Move fast. Let the journey carry you from uncertainty to action. Do not stop to perfect anything. Your goal is to understand the flow: identity, platform, discovery, audience, and strategy.

Second pass: read like a builder. After each chapter, do one small action that produces a visible output. A drafted homepage, a brand statement, a keyword list, a single published post, a simple tracking sheet, one outreach message. Small outputs compound.

If you are starting from zero, follow the chapters in order. If you already have a website and social profiles, start at the chapter that fixes your biggest leak: unclear brand, weak SEO, inconsistent content, or no plan tying it all together.

Keep one notebook or one document for this book. Create four pages inside it: Brand, Website, Content, Tracking. Every time you learn something, write it in the right page. By the end, you should have a simple operating file you can reuse.

KEY TERMS

Digital presence: the total footprint people can find online about you or your work, including your website, search results, social profiles, content, mentions, and reviews.

Brand identity: the clear signals that tell people who you are, what you stand for, who you serve, and what makes you different.

Website: your central home online where you control the message, structure, and calls to action, not a borrowed platform.

SEO (Search Engine Optimization): the practice of helping search engines understand your pages so the right people can find you through searches that match their needs.

Keyword: a word or phrase people type into search engines when they want an answer, a product, or a service.

Search intent: the reason behind a search, such as learning, comparing, or buying.

On-page SEO: improvements on your page such as titles, headings, internal links, clarity, and helpful content.

Technical SEO: site health items such as speed, mobile usability, indexing, and clean structure.

Content marketing: creating helpful content that attracts attention, builds trust, and leads people toward your offer over time.

Social media marketing: using social platforms to distribute content, build relationships, and grow attention and trust.

Call to action (CTA): a clear next step you ask the reader to take, such as subscribe, buy, book, download, or contact.

Landing page: a focused page designed to convert a visitor into a subscriber, lead, or customer.

Lead magnet: a free resource offered in exchange for an email address.

Email list: subscribers you can reach directly without relying on social algorithms.

Funnel: the steps that move a stranger into a follower, then into a customer, then into a returning customer.

Conversion: the moment a visitor completes a goal you care about, such as subscribing or buying.

Analytics: measurement tools that show what people do on your site and content so you can improve based on evidence.

KPI (Key Performance Indicator): the small set of numbers that tell you if you are improving, such as traffic, clicks, conversion rate, and revenue per page.

Chapter 1: Panyim's Design Studio

My studio has never been a quiet place.

Even when the street outside is calm, even when the city is tired and the day is folding into night, my room stays awake. Fabric does not know how to sit still. It hangs, falls, spills, and piles up like waves that refuse to return to the sea. Sketches gather on tables, on shelves, on the floor, and sometimes on the wall if I am brave enough to pin them there. Thread rolls away from me like it has its own plans. Needles appear when I am not looking, and disappear when I need them most.

That is how creation lives. It is messy. It is stubborn. It is beautiful, but it is not polite.

On that particular afternoon, the studio looked as if a storm had passed through it and decided to settle. Bolts of cloth leaned against one another like tired travelers. Swatches with daring colors pushed out of drawers. Charcoal drawings, half-finished patterns, and notes sat in uneven stacks, each stack carrying a small secret. The scent of ink, dye, and leather mixed in the air, a smell that always tells the truth about how many nights I have refused to sleep.

I stood at the center of it all, holding my old leather notebook.

That notebook is not a notebook to me. It is a witness. It has followed my hands through seasons of doubt and seasons of courage. Its spine has softened because I have opened it too many times. Its pages are not just paper. They are memory. They are the place where my ideas first became real.

Inside it, I had kept the designs for my newest collection, **Kuel**.

Kuel is a Nuer word that means *star*. I chose it on purpose, because stars have always been guides to my people. Long before a GPS, long before a phone, long before any map written in English, our eyes learned the sky. We learned direction and timing from what was above us. We learned patience from the slow movement of constellations.

So I wanted my collection to carry that same meaning. Not just clothing, but guidance. Not just style, but story.

And yet, as I flipped through those pages, the strongest feeling in my chest was not pride. It was frustration.

The designs were good. I knew they were good. I could feel it in the way the lines landed, and in the way each detail spoke to the next detail. I could see my ancestors in those strokes, even though the drawings were modern. I could sense the future in them, even though the stories were ancient.

But the world outside my studio did not know.

The world outside my studio did not care.

Or maybe it would care, if it could see what I was holding. But it could not see it. And that was the problem that kept tightening around my throat: I had a product, I had a story, I had work worth sharing, but I did not have a way for strangers to find me.

I had been told, many times, that "the internet is the answer." People said it casually, the way they say, "drink water," as if the solution is simple and universal. But nobody told me how the internet actually works for a small creator with a small budget, and a big heart, and a fear of being laughed at by people who do not understand his roots.

I stared at the notebook and thought: **How do I take what is in this room, and make it visible in the online world?**

That online world felt like an ocean. Deep. Cold. Endless. It did not feel like a place where a person could walk in with a notebook and a dream and expect to survive.

I closed the notebook and sat down for a moment, letting the silence collect. My desk lamp flickered, and the shadow of my own head moved across the paper like a warning.

Then I heard a knock at the door.

It was not a gentle knock. It was not the knock of someone who is unsure. It was sharp, certain, almost impatient. The knock of someone who believes you should answer, because something is about to change.

I did not rush to open it. I stepped carefully, weaving through fabric and sketches, moving like a man walking through his own mind, trying not to step on an idea that might matter later.

When I opened the door, the light from outside hit my face first. Then I saw her.

She stood there as if she belonged in the doorway, as if she had been standing in doorways her whole life, walking in and out of rooms where decisions were being made. Her braids were neat, and small silver accents caught the sunlight when she moved. Her posture was relaxed, but not lazy. Her eyes carried the kind of confidence that does not need to prove itself.

"Panyim?" she said, with a voice that felt light and strong at the same time.

I did not answer immediately. I have learned, in life and in business, that a man should not give his name too quickly to a stranger. Names are doors. If you open the door too early, you might let in trouble.

"That depends," I said. "Who's asking?"

She smiled, as if she expected that answer, as if she respected it.

She offered her hand. "Nyakor Akeer," she said. "Digital marketing consultant. And someone who believes the world needs to see what you've created."

I stared at her hand for a second, then shook it. Her grip was firm. Warm. Not aggressive. Just honest.

"Digital marketing?" I repeated, tasting the words like food I was not sure I would like.

She laughed softly. "Think of it as the bridge between your masterpiece and the people searching for it. Right now, your art is a hidden gem. I want to make sure the right eyes find it."

A bridge.

That word caught me. Because a bridge makes sense to me. A bridge is not magic. It is built. It is tested. It carries weight. It connects two places that were once separated.

I looked back into my studio, and my eyes landed on a spool of thread that had rolled near my foot earlier. It sat there, stopped, as if it also was waiting for a decision. I understood the picture without explaining it: I had been working with thread my whole life, but I had not threaded my work into the world.

"The online world feels… overwhelming," I admitted. "Like a beast too large to tame."

Nyakor stepped closer, not into my space, but into the moment. "Perhaps," she said. "But what if that beast could carry your designs across the world?"

That question stayed in my chest.

Because it is one thing to fear the internet. It is another thing to imagine the internet as a vehicle instead of a threat.

I breathed in, slowly, and I felt something I had not felt all day: a small spark of readiness.

"Alright," I said. "Show me how to turn this beast into an ally."

Nyakor's smile widened, like she had been waiting for that exact sentence.

"That's the spirit," she said. "Let's make Kuel a star that shines beyond the digital sky."

And just like that, my studio stopped being only a studio.

It became the first classroom.

What I Want You to Learn From My Studio

Before I continue the story, I want to teach you what my studio taught me, because your "studio" might not look like mine.

Your studio might be a small desk in a rented room. It might be a phone with a cracked screen. It might be a kitchen where you bake cakes for neighbors. It might be a laptop where you design logos at midnight. It might be a notebook where you write poems that nobody has read yet.

Whatever it is, the first lesson is this:

Digital marketing does not start online. It starts where the work is made.

If you skip that truth, you will build a shiny online presence around something weak, unclear, or confusing. Then you will wonder why people click and do not buy, or follow and do not trust, or visit and never return.

So here is what I did in my studio, and what I want you to do in yours.

Lesson 1: Your Work Must Be Clear Before Your Marketing Can Be Clear

Nyakor looked at my mess and did not panic. She did not judge. She walked in and felt possibility.

Then she did something important: she asked questions.

She picked up one sketch, then another. She asked what each piece meant. She asked what story it carried.

That is not a small detail. That is marketing.

Marketing is not shouting. Marketing is clarity.

When you cannot explain your offer clearly, you will not be able to sell it clearly. When you cannot name your value, you will not be able to communicate it. When your work has meaning but your message is silent, people will scroll past you without even knowing what they missed.

So I started by answering Nyakor's questions.

I told her the story behind my designs. I spoke about stars as guides. I spoke about the strength of women. I spoke about unity.

As I spoke, something happened. I began to hear my own story more clearly. I began to see what I was truly selling.

I was not selling cloth.

I was selling identity made visible.

I was selling belonging that people could wear.

I was selling beauty with a message.

You might be selling something else. But you still need this moment where you can say, in plain words, what your product is and why it matters.

My studio exercise for you

Write a simple statement and do not overthink it:

- **I create:** (what you make)
- **For:** (who it is for)
- **So they can:** (the result they want)
- **Because I believe:** (your driving reason)

Example from my studio could sound like this:

I create fashion designs rooted in cultural heritage for people who want style with meaning, so they can wear beauty that carries a story, because I believe identity should be honored, not hidden.

That statement is not decoration. It is direction.

When you have direction, you can choose platforms, content, and campaigns that match your real purpose.

Lesson 2: Your Brand Story Is Not a Speech, It Is a Thread

When Nyakor said, "It's not just fashion; it's storytelling in fabric," she was naming what makes people care.

People do not connect to products first. They connect to meaning. Then they buy the product as a way to hold that meaning in their hands.

So I learned to treat story as thread.

A thread does not scream. It pulls quietly. It connects pieces. It holds the shape together.

Your story should do the same.

Here is what that means in practice:

- Your story should show where your work comes from.
- Your story should show what you stand for.
- Your story should show what problem you solve.
- Your story should show why you are different from the next person selling something similar.
- Your story should show what kind of person your customer becomes when they buy from you.

If you cannot put those points into sentences, you do not need better ads. You need better story.

A simple story pattern I use

I use this pattern because it keeps me honest:

1. **Origin:** where did this begin for me?
2. **Struggle:** what was hard, and what did it teach me?
3. **Decision:** what choice did I make that changed my path?
4. **Promise:** what do I now promise the customer?
5. **Proof:** what can I show that supports this promise?

This is not theory. This is how I speak when I write captions, when I write product pages, and when I talk in a video.

When you repeat your story in a consistent way, people begin to recognize you. Recognition becomes trust. Trust becomes sales.

Lesson 3: The Internet Does Not Reward Perfection, It Rewards Presence

I used to believe I needed to polish everything before I showed anything.

That belief feels noble, but it is a trap.

Nyakor did not walk into my studio and tell me to perfect more. She walked in and told me to be seen.

And she was right.

The internet rewards those who show up, who publish, who learn, who adjust, who keep moving.

If you wait until you are "ready," you will remain invisible.

So I made a decision that day: I would treat the online world as a place to practice, not a place to perform.

That shift changed everything.

It freed me from fear.

It made me willing to post the first photo, even if the lighting was not perfect.

It made me willing to write the first caption, even if the wording was not poetic.

It made me willing to build the first page of the website, even if I later changed the design.

If you learn only one thing from this chapter, let it be this:

Your first job online is to exist clearly.

Lesson 4: Your First Digital Asset Is Not a Website, It Is Your Identity

Nyakor said, "First, a logo. Something that embodies Kuel's essence."

That is the right order.

Many people rush to build websites and social pages before they know what they want those pages to say.

A logo is not the whole brand, but it forces you to decide something: shape, symbol, feeling, meaning.

In my case, I pulled out a sketch of a stylized Nuer woman reaching for a star. When Nyakor saw it, she knew it was right.

Why?

Because it carried the heart of the brand in one image.

That is what your first digital asset should do. Not impress everyone. Just capture the heart.

What you need in the beginning

You do not need a full design system. You need a small set of decisions:

- Your brand name
- A simple logo or mark
- Two brand colors you can repeat
- One font style you use consistently
- A short brand statement (the one you wrote earlier)
- A small photo set that matches your style (even if taken with a phone)

That is enough to start building. Anything beyond that can come later.

Lesson 5: Your Digital Presence Has a Home Base

When Nyakor said, "Social media, a website, a home for Kuel beyond these walls," she was teaching me a principle: you need a home base.

Social media is rented land. It can change rules overnight. It can hide your posts. It can lock your account. It can make you feel like you are working hard for nothing.

A website is owned land. It is where your story lives permanently. It is where your products can be found without scrolling. It is where your brand can breathe.

So I learned to think like this:

- **Website:** the home base
- **Social platforms:** the roads that bring people home

That idea is simple, but it saves you from chasing every trend.

If you only build on social media, you are building your house on someone else's ground. If they decide to remove you, your whole structure collapses.

So from the start, I decided my website would be my anchor.

Lesson 6: Your First Marketing Plan Should Fit Your Life, Not Your Fantasy

A lot of digital marketing advice assumes you have money, time, and a team.

I did not.

My studio was already demanding. My energy was limited. My budget was real. My fears were real.

So Nyakor and I did not plan a huge campaign on day one. We planned what we could actually do.

That is what I want you to do.

A plan that fits your life is better than a plan you cannot sustain.

My "minimum plan" rule

I follow a simple rule:

Choose the smallest set of actions you can repeat weekly for six months.

If you can do that, you will win.

Because six months of consistent effort beats two weeks of excitement followed by silence.

Here is an example of a minimum plan that works for many creators:

- One website page improved each week
- Two social posts per week
- One short video per week (even 30 seconds)
- Ten minutes of engagement per day (reply, comment, connect)
- One outreach message per week (partner, blogger, customer, friend)

That is not glamorous. But it is workable.

And workable is what brings results.

The Studio Audit: What You Should Do Today

Before we ended that first meeting, Nyakor and I looked around the studio and made a decision: we would not market confusion.

We would market clarity.

So we did a studio audit.

I want you to do the same.

Step A: List your "products" clearly

Write what you actually sell. Not what you hope to sell.

- Product or service name
- What it includes
- Price range
- Who it is for
- The main result it gives

If you have too many things, start with one. The internet rewards focus, especially in the beginning.

Step B: Gather proof

Proof is not bragging. Proof is respect for the buyer.

Proof can be:

- photos of your work
- testimonials
- before-and-after results
- a short story of a customer
- behind-the-scenes process
- your personal journey that shows credibility

If you have no proof yet, start making it. Document your process. Show your work in progress. Let people see your hands. Trust grows when people see reality.

Step C: Identify the first audience you can actually reach

Do not aim for "everyone."

Who are the first people who are most likely to care?

In my case, it was people who love fashion and also love culture, meaning, and story. It was not every fashion buyer on the planet. It was a specific kind of buyer.

Your first audience might be:

- people in your city
- people from your community
- people who already follow similar creators
- people who are searching for a specific problem you solve

Start there. Build a base. Expand later.

Step D: Choose your first two platforms

Pick:

- one home base (website)
- one main social platform (where your buyers already spend time)

You can add more later, but start with two.

When you start with too many platforms, you spread yourself thin and then blame marketing when the real problem was focus.

Back to the Story: Nyakor Walks In

Nyakor stepped into my studio fully. Her presence shifted the air in a way I cannot explain with logic. It felt like possibility had entered and refused to leave.

She did not ask me first how many followers I had.

She did not ask me first how much money I had.

She did not ask me first how popular I was.

She asked about the work.

"This," she said, touching a sketch gently, "is stunning. It's storytelling in fabric."

I straightened, because every creator knows what it means when someone sees the work, not just the product.

"Tell me about this one," she said, holding a drawing as if it were fragile. "What story does it hold?"

I breathed out slowly. The tension I had been carrying loosened a little.

And I began to explain.

As I spoke, I realized something: I had been hiding my story from the world, but I had also been hiding it from my marketing.

I had not been telling people enough to help them understand why they should care.

Nyakor listened, nodded, and then said words that I still remember clearly:

"These are powerful stories, Panyim. People will connect with them. But they need to hear them first."

That sentence was a mirror.

I had been asking, "What if they reject me?"

But the real question was, "What if they never even hear me?"

The fear of rejection is loud, but the danger of silence is worse.

So when Nyakor asked what worried me most, I did not pretend.

"I don't know how to start," I told her.

She smiled, and the smile had two messages inside it: kindness and certainty.

"That's where I come in," she said. "We'll carve a path, find the people who need to see this."

I raised my eyebrow, still skeptical, because skepticism is a shield when you are afraid.

"Through Twitter threads and Instagram posts?" I asked.

Nyakor laughed. "Exactly. Social media, a website, a home for Kuel beyond these walls."

Then my fear spoke again.

"What if nobody likes it?" I said. "What if they think my designs are strange?"

Nyakor looked at me in a way that made it hard to lie to myself.

"The right people will see the beauty," she said. "You don't have to hide your heritage. You should embrace it. That's your strength."

That was the moment the studio changed.

Not because my fabric changed.

Not because my sketches changed.

But because my thinking changed.

I had been treating my heritage like a risk. Nyakor treated it like an advantage.

And if you want to win in digital marketing, you need that shift too.

Because the internet is full of copies.

The only thing that cannot be copied is your honest identity.

I looked at her and nodded.

"Alright," I said. "What happens next?"

Nyakor clapped her hands once, like a person beginning serious work.

"First," she said, "a logo."

And for the first time, instead of feeling like the online world was a beast, I felt like it was a road.

A road that could carry my work.

A road that could carry my story.

A road that could carry my star.

Chapter 1 Notes From Me to You

Before you go to Chapter 2, I want you to hold these points:

1) Your studio is enough to start.
Do not wait for perfect conditions. Start with what you have.

2) Clarity comes before clicks.
A clear offer and a clear story beat loud promotion.

3) Your heritage, your personality, your approach, your lived experience are not a weakness.
They are the reason people will remember you.

4) Choose a home base.
Build something you own, even if it starts small.

5) Consistency is a form of respect.
Respect your future self. Respect your future customer. Show up.

In the next chapter, you will see what happened to me the moment I stopped being only a creator and began acting like a brand owner.

Chapter 2: Panyim Expresses His Excitement

I am going to tell you a truth that most people hide behind "confidence" posts and polished brand photos.

Even when you know your work is good, putting it in front of people can shake you.

It is nerve-wracking to launch a product, publish a blog post, record a video, pitch a partnership, or stand in a room and explain your idea. Self-doubt does not ask for permission. It walks in, sits down, and starts talking as if it owns the place.

But I have also learned something else.

Excitement can beat fear, if you learn how to guide it.

In Chapter 1, I was building. I was sketching, shaping, and trying to make my work visible. Now I want to show you what happens when the first real moment arrives. The moment you realize people can actually see you. The moment your heart jumps. The moment your hands shake. The moment you say, "This is real."

That moment is not just emotional. It is also a business moment.

It is the moment where most creators either shrink back into hiding, or step forward and start building a real digital presence.

This chapter is about stepping forward.

It is about excitement, yes, but not the childish excitement that burns out in one day. I mean disciplined excitement. The kind that can carry a brand through criticism, slow days, and the long middle where nobody claps.

I will use stories to teach you because stories make lessons stick. The characters are examples, but the pressures are real.

Scene 1: The Waiting Room That Teaches You Everything

I still remember the day I was scheduled to present my clothing line, *Nile Threads*, to **Abeni Mensah**, a legend in business consulting.

I had poured my heart into each design. I had stitched culture into cloth. I had taken ideas that lived in my head and made them wearable. Yet I sat in that waiting room as if I had done nothing.

The clock did not help. Every tick sounded like a judge.

In digital marketing, this is what a launch feels like.

You can build the site.
You can write the copy.
You can plan the content.
You can schedule the posts.

But when it is time to publish, your body reacts like you are about to walk into a courtroom.

That is why many people keep "preparing" forever.

They call it strategy, but sometimes it is fear dressed in professional language.

Then **Nyakor** walked in.

She was confident in a way that made you stand straighter without trying. She brought my favorite street food, spicy beef skewers, and just the smell reminded me that I was not alone.

She said something simple that landed like a brick in my mind:

"Ms. Abeni wouldn't have agreed to see you if your designs weren't something special."

That line did two things.

It calmed me, and it pushed me.

It reminded me that the opportunity itself was evidence.

In marketing, you need that reminder.

If someone clicked your link, that is evidence.
If someone read your post to the end, that is evidence.
If someone saved your pin, that is evidence.
If someone replied to your email, that is evidence.

You do not need a million people to prove your work matters. You need one real signal and the courage to keep going.

Nyakor taught me a crucial lesson that day: surround yourself with people who believe in you, because their belief can hold you steady when yours is shaking.

That is not just emotional support. It is a marketing advantage.

Creators with no support often quit at the first wave of silence.

Creators with support publish again.

And publishing again is how brands are born.

Lesson 1: Turn Fear Into a Presentation You Can Repeat

That day also taught me something practical.

Fear gets worse when your message is vague.

Confidence grows when your message becomes specific.

So I started preparing differently.

Not by adding more "motivation," but by adding structure.

The book's original takeaway says it plainly: preparation is key, lean on your support system, and reframe nervous energy as excitement.

I agree, and I want to make it usable.

My "Three-Page Presentation" Method

When I am afraid to present, I reduce the whole thing to three pages.

Page 1: The Promise

- What am I offering?
- Who is it for?
- What changes for them if it works?

Page 2: The Proof

- What have I already done that shows I can deliver?
- What results, examples, or process can I point to?
- What story demonstrates it?

Page 3: The Path

- What happens next if they say yes?
- What is the first step?
- What is the simplest way to begin?

If you can answer those three pages, you can pitch.
You can write a landing page.
You can record a video.
You can introduce your product on social media.

And you can repeat it without reinventing your identity every week.

That is the difference between hype and a real message.

Digital Marketing Application

If you are building a digital presence, you will present constantly:

- You will present in captions.
- You will present in emails.
- You will present on your homepage.
- You will present in DMs.
- You will present in comments when people question your credibility.

So treat presentation like a skill, not a one-time event.

Scene 2: The Publish Button That Feels Like a Cliff

Let me take you back to the studio.

In the story, the studio is alive with fabric, machines, beads, and heritage. Then the digital side begins. A website post goes live. A blog becomes the heartbeat of the brand.

Nyakor hesitates for a moment, then hits "publish."

That small moment is bigger than it looks.

Because "publish" is where creators change categories.

Before publish: you are "working on it."
After publish: you are in the market.

Even if nobody sees it on day one, you have crossed a line.

Then something happens.

A message arrives:

Someone says the designs are breathtaking.
Someone says the story is powerful.

Someone says they did not know anything about the Nuer people, but now they are hooked.

And I feel something shift. I turn to Nyakor and I say, "People want to hear our stories."

That is the excitement.

That is what this chapter is named for.

But excitement is not the finish line.

It is the ignition.

If you do not guide it, it becomes anxiety.

If you guide it, it becomes consistency.

Lesson 2: Excitement Is a Signal, Not a Plan

Here is a mistake I have made, and I have watched others make it too.

You get one good comment, one good week, one good spike.

Then you assume the road is now easy.

But the road is not easy yet.

The road is simply visible now.

That first positive signal should tell you one thing:

Your message is landing somewhere.

Now your job is to turn that "somewhere" into a system.

The System That Turns Excitement Into Growth

When I feel that rush, I do four things immediately:

1) I capture the signal

- Screenshot the comment.
- Save the email.
- Note the words they used.

2) I name what worked

- Was it the story?
- Was it the photo?
- Was it the headline?
- Was it the clarity?

3) I repeat the core, not the exact post

- Same theme, new angle.
- Same promise, new story.
- Same audience, new entry point.

4) I decide the next publish date
Not "when I feel inspired."
A date.

Because when excitement fades, the calendar still stands.

This is how you train your brand to move even when your feelings change.

Scene 3: Criticism Arrives, and You Learn What You Are Made Of

Praise came, and then criticism came.

A comment hits like a slap:

"Another cultural appropriation attempt? These clothes are just cheap knock-offs trying to capitalize on trends."

In that moment, everything in me wants to react.

This is what happens online.

If you are doing real work, you will be misunderstood.
If you are visible, you will be judged.
If you are building something meaningful, someone will try to reduce it into something ugly.

Nyakor stays calm. She tells me not to let it get to me. She reminds me this is also about how we respond and how we educate.

So I write a response.

Not defensive.
Not weak.
Clear.

I explain what the brand is.
I explain fair pay.
I explain story.
I explain heritage.

And then something unexpected happens.

By morning, the comment section shifts into dialogue. Support comes in. People praise the response. Engagement deepens.

That is a marketing lesson.

Not the shallow kind.

A serious one:

How you respond becomes part of your brand.

Lesson 3: Your Response Strategy Is Part of Your Content Strategy

Most people think content is:

- Posts
- Videos
- Blogs
- Emails

But in real life, content also includes:

- Your replies
- Your tone under pressure
- Your public boundaries
- Your clarity when accused
- Your ability to teach without insulting

If you do not plan your response strategy, you will build it in panic.

My Response Framework

When criticism hits, I ask:

1) Is this a real concern or a troll?

- If troll: ignore or delete depending on platform rules.
- If real concern: respond once, clearly.

2) Can I teach something here?
If yes, I teach.
If no, I keep it short.

3) What values must show up in my response?
For me:

- Respect
- Truth

- Dignity
- Clarity

This is not just "reputation management."

It is trust-building.

And trust is what carries a brand longer than viral posts ever will.

Scene 4: The Creative Block That Comes After Success

Now let's talk about a quieter enemy.

Sometimes the fear is not public criticism.

Sometimes the fear is silence in your own head.

The book describes it clearly: staring at blank pages, feeling like inspiration left, slumped at a desk, and a friend named **Ethan** urging a change of perspective.

Then an ordinary object helps. An antique telescope sparks an idea. Suddenly creativity returns.

That is not just a writing story.

That is a marketing story.

Because content creation is not a straight line.

You will have seasons where you produce easily.

Then you will hit a wall.

If you do not have a method for those walls, you will disappear for months.

And disappearing is expensive.

Not only in traffic and sales, but in trust.

Lesson 4: Build a "Creative Recovery" Routine

Here is the practical takeaway in the manuscript: Step away, change environment, collaborate, and find inspiration in ordinary things.

Now let me turn it into a routine you can repeat.

My 30-Minute Creative Recovery Routine

When I feel stuck, I do this:

Minute 1 to 10: Move
Walk. Stretch. Wash dishes. Anything physical.

Minute 11 to 20: Collect
I collect three things:

- one photo
- one phrase
- one question

Minute 21 to 30: Connect
I connect one of those things to my audience's problem.

That is it.

I do not force a masterpiece.

I just create the next usable piece:

- a short post
- a quick email
- a rough outline
- a voice note script

Then I publish something small.

That small publish keeps the engine warm.

Scene 5: Visibility Does Not Happen Overnight, So You Must Become Patient on Purpose

The manuscript says it plainly.

Panyim faced the fear of visibility. With countless brands online, he wondered if his work would ever be discovered.

So he took calculated risks:

- reached out to influencers
- pitched to local boutiques
- built a brand story
- stayed persistent even when visibility was slow

That is one of the most realistic things in the whole chapter.

Because success does not arrive like a dramatic movie scene for most people.

It arrives like this:

- one small audience
- then two
- then a few returning people
- then someone shares
- then someone writes about you
- then one day you look back and realize you are no longer invisible

If you quit early, you never reach the part where compounding begins.

Lesson 5: Risk Is Required, but It Must Be Chosen

The manuscript's takeaway is:
Be proactive, tell a compelling story, accept uncertainty.

I agree, and I want to make it more concrete.

The "Three Risks" Rule

I take three kinds of risks, on purpose.

1) Audience risk
I publish something honest instead of something safe.

2) Outreach risk
I message someone bigger than me, respectfully, without begging.

3) Offer risk
I ask for the sale, the signup, the meeting, the collaboration.

If I am doing none of these, I am probably hiding.

If I am doing all of these recklessly, I will burn out.

So I keep it at three.

Then I repeat weekly.

That is how you grow without turning your life into panic.

Lesson 6: Use Self-Doubt as Fuel, Not as a Judge

Self-doubt is inevitable.

The manuscript says I learned to turn it into a tool: I remember late nights, revisit earlier drafts, prepare better, refine craft, and push forward.

Let me add what I do in practice.

The Self-Doubt Audit

When doubt shows up, I ask:

What is doubt trying to protect me from?

- embarrassment?
- rejection?
- being misunderstood?
- being seen?

Then I respond with action, not argument.

If the fear is embarrassment, I practice.
If the fear is rejection, I publish anyway.
If the fear is misunderstanding, I tighten my message.
If the fear is being seen, I remember that hiding has a cost.

This is what mature digital marketing looks like.

Not loud.
Not frantic.
Clear.

Putting It Into Digital Marketing Language

Let me translate the entire chapter into plain digital marketing terms.

Facing the fear of presentation is:

- writing a landing page without hiding behind vague words
- pitching your offer clearly
- recording your first video without waiting for perfection

Overcoming creative block is:

- building a recovery routine so content does not depend on mood

Embracing risk and uncertainty is:

- outreach
- partnerships
- publishing consistently before you are famous

Using self-doubt as motivation is:

- documenting progress
- improving one thing at a time
- remembering why you started

This is how excitement becomes growth.

Exercises: What I Want You to Do After This Chapter
Exercise 1: Write Your Three-Page Presentation

- Promise
- Proof
- Path

Do it in one sitting.
Messy is fine.
Clear is the goal.

Exercise 2: Publish Something Small in 24 Hours

Not a masterpiece.
Something small that serves your audience:

- one short story
- one lesson
- one tip
- one example
- one before-and-after

Exercise 3: Plan Your First Response

Write a short response you will use when someone questions you:

- about your credibility
- about your pricing
- about your identity
- about your right to speak

Keep it respectful.
Keep it clear.
Keep it anchored in values.

Exercise 4: Build Your Creative Recovery Routine

Pick your version:

- 30 minutes daily
- or 60 minutes twice a week

The goal is simple:
When you get stuck, you do not disappear.

Closing: The Real Reward Is Who You Become

The manuscript ends with a reminder that the journey itself is where growth happens, and it asks a direct question: what is your next big idea, and when will you take the leap?

I will ask you the same, but in my own words.

What have you been holding back because you are waiting to "feel ready"?

And what would happen if you treated readiness as something you build through action?

Because excitement is not a gift that only visits a few people.

It is a signal.

It is your inner life telling you, "There is something here."

Your job is to take that signal seriously, shape it into a message, publish it, and keep going long after the first rush fades.

That is how digital marketing success begins.

That is how your digital presence becomes real.

Chapter 3: The Concept of Digital Presence

I remember the first time I truly questioned my presence online. I was not working. I was not learning. I was not even thinking. I was just scrolling, the way people scroll when they want to rest, but end up restless. My feed was full of perfectly framed travel photos, meals plated like art, and influencers praising products I had never heard of. And somewhere between those glowing images, a familiar feeling started rising in me.

Not jealousy.

Something quieter and more poisonous.

A feeling that maybe my life was not "enough."

I mumbled to Nyakor, "Everyone seems to be living these amazing lives."

She did not even hesitate. She looked up from her worn leather notebook and smiled like someone who had seen this trap many times.

"Curated, not real," she said. "Social media is a highlight reel, not a documentary of someone's actual existence."

That line struck me hard, because it was simple and true.

Then I looked at my own profile. It was a neglected wasteland of blurry childhood photos and random quotes. I had never seriously thought about what my digital presence said about me. But now I could not unsee it.

If someone searched my name, what would they learn?

If someone visited my profile, what would they believe?

If someone discovered my work, would they trust me enough to follow, subscribe, or buy?

Nyakor tilted her head and challenged me, playful but serious.

"Maybe it's time you did," she said. "The world needs to see what you have to offer. Not just your friends and family, but people who share your passions."

That conversation became a turning point. I began to understand that digital presence is not a beauty contest. It is not a race for attention. It is not a place to perform a fake life.

Digital presence is a bridge.

A bridge between who you are, what you do, and the people who need it.

And if you build that bridge the right way, it becomes more than visibility. It becomes connection, community, and opportunity.

What Digital Presence Really Means

When I say *digital presence*, I mean this:

Your digital presence is what people learn about you when they meet you online.

Sometimes they meet you on purpose, because they searched your name.

Sometimes they meet you by accident, because a friend shared your post.

Either way, they start forming a conclusion before they ever speak to you.

That conclusion usually comes from five places:

1) Your identity signals
Your name, photo, bio, brand colors, tone, and the "first impression" of your profiles.

2) Your proof signals
Your work samples, posts, testimonials, comments, collaborations, and consistency.

3) Your trust signals
How you speak, how you respond under pressure, how you treat people, what you stand for.

4) Your value signals
Whether you educate, entertain, inspire, solve problems, or waste time.

5) Your connection signals
Whether you engage, listen, reply, and treat people like humans instead of numbers.

Most people think digital presence equals "posting." That is a small part.

Digital presence is the full picture people receive.

And that full picture can either open doors for you or quietly shut them.

The Two Sides of Digital Presence: What You Control and What You Must Manage

Nyakor taught me early that digital presence has two sides.

The side you control

- your website
- your email list
- your content library

- your offers
- your profile pages
- your brand story

The side you must manage

- comments
- reviews
- search results
- rumors
- misunderstandings
- old posts that still surface

The smart creator builds controlled assets first, then uses social platforms as distribution.

Nyakor said it best in her own way when she explained that a brand needs a home, a website that captures its essence, a place where people experience your work, not just glance at it.

A website is not just a page. It is your base.

And social media is not your base. It is your megaphone.

I did not fully understand that at first. But once I did, my thinking changed.

The First Trap: Comparison That Kills Authenticity

Let me say this clearly.

Scrolling can teach you.

But scrolling can also poison you.

If your digital presence is built from comparison, it will always feel unstable. Today you feel inspired, tomorrow you feel small. Today you love your work, tomorrow you question it. That instability makes people inconsistent, and inconsistency makes people invisible.

Nyakor's "curated, not real" reminder saved me from building a fake personality.

Because the easiest way to fail online is to build a brand you cannot sustain.

If you build a brand that requires you to pretend, you will burn out.

If you build a brand that requires you to copy others, you will always look like a weaker version of someone else.

If you build a brand from truth, you can keep showing up.

So the first rule of digital presence is not "post more."

The first rule is:

Build something you can live inside.

Step 1: Identifying Your Passion

Nyakor's first question was simple, but it went straight to the root.

"What makes your soul sing?"

Without hesitation, I answered: **music**. Specifically, the **djembe**. The rhythm, the power, the cultural depth. It had always been part of me.

She nodded.

"That's where we start," she said. "But it's not just about playing the djembe. What's the story behind it? Why does it matter to you?"

That question forced me to go deeper than "what I like."

It forced me to find meaning.

I realized my uncle introduced me to the djembe when I was a child. He was a master drummer, weaving rhythms like stories told without words. That connection was not a detail. It was the foundation of my voice.

So here is what I want you to learn from my moment:

Your passion becomes powerful online when it has a story.

People do not only follow skills.

They follow meaning.

Exercise: Your Passion Map

Write down answers to these:

- What do I talk about for hours without getting tired?
- What do I return to even when life is hard?
- Who introduced me to it, and how?
- What personal memory carries the emotion of it?
- What problem can I help others solve through it?

This is not busywork. This is your foundation.

And Nyakor's actionable tip is exactly right: write these down, because they form the base of your digital presence.

Step 2: Creating Authentic Content

Once I knew what I was about, Nyakor gave me the second rule.

Authenticity.

Not "look professional."

Not "sound clever."

Authenticity.

She explained it again later when she told me to share my process, the late nights, the breakthroughs, the inspiration behind each piece, and to let people see the artist behind the brand.

That advice applies to every field, not only fashion.

If you want a real digital presence, you cannot only show polished results.

You must show your hands.

You must show your human side.

You must show the work behind the work.

The book says it plainly: you do not need to be perfect, and sharing behind-the-scenes moments builds trust, and trust builds loyalty.

I agree, and I want to make it practical.

What Authentic Content Looks Like

Authentic content includes:

- behind-the-scenes steps
- mistakes you learned from
- "before and after" progress
- reasons behind your decisions
- lessons you learned the hard way
- the story behind your product, not only the product

It is not oversharing your whole life.

It is sharing what serves your audience.

A person does not trust you because you look perfect.

A person trusts you because you look real and consistent.

Step 3: Choosing the Right Platforms

After I started building content, I wanted to be everywhere.

Nyakor stopped me.

"Where does your audience spend most of their time?" she asked.

So I researched.

And I found my ideal customers were on **Instagram, TikTok, and YouTube,** platforms that thrive on visual storytelling. That discovery helped me focus, instead of spreading myself too thin across every platform.

That one decision can save you years of frustration.

Because platform choice is not about popularity. It is about fit.

- Visual creators often thrive on Instagram and Pinterest.
- Storytellers can thrive on blogging, podcasting, and long-form video.
- Teachers can thrive on YouTube, newsletters, and searchable content.

My Platform Rule

Pick **one home platform** and **one supporting platform**.

- Home platform: where you can explain and build depth.
- Supporting platform: where you can distribute and attract new people.

You can add more later, but only after you can maintain consistency.

Step 4: Creating a Content Calendar

This is where many excited creators collapse.

They post randomly.

One week they post every day.

Then they disappear for a month.

That was me too, until Nyakor made me see the truth: consistency is key, and we created a simple content calendar with themes for each week.

Then she showed me a schedule example that was simple and realistic:

- Monday: a behind-the-scenes video
- Wednesday: a styling tip post
- Friday: a customer story or testimonial
- Sunday: a live Q&A session

That is not a prison. That is freedom.

Because you do not wake up every day asking, "What should I post?"

You already decided.

My "Theme Week" Method

I build weeks around one theme.

Example themes:

- "Beginner week"
- "Behind the scenes week"
- "Mistakes week"
- "Tools week"
- "Customer story week"

Then each post becomes a different angle of the same theme.

This makes content creation easier, and it also trains your audience to know what you are about.

Step 5: Engaging With Your Audience

At first, I thought engagement meant talking.

Nyakor corrected me.

She said social media is a conversation, and that I should listen first, read comments and messages, because it is a two-way street.

That changed everything for me.

Because engagement is not "likes."

Engagement is relationship.

When you reply, you signal that a real person is here.

When you ask questions, you invite people into your journey.

When you feature user-generated content, you honor your community.

The book's step says it clearly: creating content was not enough, I had to interact, respond to comments, ask for feedback, and share user content so people felt part of my journey.

This is not optional if you want a strong digital presence.

A brand without conversation feels cold.

A brand with conversation becomes human.

The Engagement Habits I Practice

Here are habits I use:

- reply to comments within 24 hours when possible
- pin thoughtful comments
- thank people by name when they support
- ask one question in captions to invite response
- take feedback seriously without becoming controlled by it

You do not need to reply to everything.

But you must reply enough to prove you are present.

Step 6: Measuring Success and Adapting

Nyakor introduced me to analytics when momentum started building.

"Tracking your progress helps you refine your strategy," she said.

So we started paying attention.

After a few months, I noticed some posts performed better than others. We analyzed engagement data and adjusted. If a format worked well, we created more of it. If something fell flat, we tweaked it.

This is what separates hobby posting from business building.

The Metrics That Actually Matter

I track these:

1) Reach
Are new people seeing the work?

2) Engagement quality
Are people saving, sharing, commenting, replying?

3) Conversion
Are people clicking, subscribing, buying, booking, or taking the next step?

4) Retention
Are people coming back?

5) Community signals
Are people speaking about you when you are not in the room?

Vanity numbers can feel good, but they can also distract you.

I would rather have 200 people who trust me than 20,000 people who forget me tomorrow.

The Digital Presence Stack: Home, Megaphone, and Story

At some point, Nyakor sat with me and laid it out simply.

Your brand needs a home. A website that showcases your work, tells your story, and makes it easy to connect.

Social media is your megaphone. It is how you engage, intrigue, and inspire people.

Storytelling is your glue. It turns posts into meaning.

The manuscript even puts it like a crown: content is king, and storytelling is its crown.

I like that, because it is not just poetic. It is practical.

If your website is strong but your social media is silent, growth becomes slow.

If your social media is loud but you have no website or home base, you live at the mercy of platforms and trends.

If you have both, and you can tell a story, you become hard to ignore.

A Real Example: How I Would Build Digital Presence From Zero Today

If I was starting again, this is exactly what I would do.

Week 1: Foundation

- choose one clear niche tied to passion and story
- write a simple bio that says who I help and why
- clean up profiles: photo, headline, link, short story

Week 2: First Content Batch

- write 10 post ideas from my story
- record 3 short videos showing process
- create 1 long-form piece explaining my "why"

Week 3: Calendar and Engagement

- build a realistic weekly schedule
- commit to consistency
- start replying and listening

Week 4: Measurement

- review what worked
- double down on formats that perform
- improve one thing at a time

That is it.

Not flashy.

Not complicated.

But it works because it is sustainable.

Common Mistakes I See and How I Fix Them
Mistake 1: Posting Without a Center

Fix: define your passion and story first.

Mistake 2: Trying to Impress Instead of Connect

Fix: create authentic content and show the process.

Mistake 3: Being Everywhere

Fix: choose platforms based on audience, not ego.

Mistake 4: No Calendar

Fix: use a schedule you can keep.

Mistake 5: Talking Without Listening

Fix: engagement starts with listening and replying.

Mistake 6: Ignoring Data

Fix: measure, adapt, repeat.

Closing: Digital Presence Is Not a Mask, It Is a Mirror

By the end of that first conversation with Nyakor, I realized something that sounds simple but changes everything.

Digital presence is not about becoming someone else.

It is about becoming visible as yourself, with clarity.

If your presence is honest, it attracts the right people.

If your presence is consistent, it earns trust.

If your presence is useful, it creates impact.

And if your presence is built on story, it becomes unforgettable.

Nyakor was right. Social media can be more than comparison. It can be a space to connect, share, and build a community.

So now I will ask you to take one action today:

Write down your passion, your story, and your audience. Then publish one authentic piece that proves you are present.

You do not need to be perfect.

You need to be real, consistent, and willing to be seen.

Chapter 4: The Importance of a Website

I used to think a website was optional.

I believed what many creators believe at the beginning, that if you post consistently on social media, people will find you, follow you, and buy. Social media felt alive. It felt like a marketplace with noise, movement, and instant reaction. A website, on the other hand, felt like a quiet building on an empty street. Why build a house when the crowd is already dancing in the public square?

Then I learned the hard truth.

The public square can change its rules without warning. The crowd can move. The gatekeepers can silence you, bury you, or misread you. And even when things are going well, social media is still not your home. It is someone else's property.

That is why a website matters.

When I first asked Nyakor whether I really needed a website, she did not treat my question as foolish. She treated it as normal, the same way a designer asks whether they need a second sewing machine, or whether they can keep stitching by hand forever. She reminded me that a website is not just another marketing channel. It is your storefront, your credibility, and your center of gravity.

And once I accepted that, I stopped seeing a website as a technical project. I started seeing it as the place where my brand learns to stand on its own legs.

A website is not a brochure, it is a home

A brochure says, "Here is what I do."

A home says, "Welcome. Stay a bit. Let me show you who I am, what I make, what I believe, and how you can walk with me."

That is what a website becomes when you build it well.

Nyakor described it in a way that stayed with me. She told me my brand needed a home, a website that captures its essence, where people do not only see the work but experience it. That word, *experience*, changed everything for me. Because experience is where trust begins, and trust is where business begins.

If your website is built with intention, it becomes:

A place to tell your story in full. Social media gives you fragments. Your website gives you the full narrative, written the way you mean it.

A place to guide the buyer. Social platforms love distraction. Your website can be focused and calm, like a good shop where each step makes sense.

A place to collect relationships. Followers are not relationships. Email subscribers, customers, clients, readers, and community members are closer to relationships, because you can speak to them directly.

A place to be found through search. Social media is mostly a feed. Search is a library. When your pages show up in search, people find you while they are already looking for what you offer.

A place you can improve week by week. A good website is never finished. It is refined. You can update pages, improve clarity, test messaging, improve speed, and fix what is broken.

And the moment I saw all that, I stopped asking, "Do I need a website?" and started asking, "What kind of website do I need?"

The website and the public square

I still use social media. I still value it. I still respect its power.

But I now treat social media like a road that leads people home, not like the home itself.

In practice, that changes how I work:

I post content on social media, but each post has a purpose. It points somewhere. It invites people into something deeper. It leads to a page, a post, a product, a signup, or a story.

Nyakor used a simple line that I repeat to myself whenever I feel tempted to build only for the feed: *your website is your storefront.*

A storefront has to be welcoming. It has to be easy to move around in. It has to be organized. It has to be honest. It has to show what you sell. And it has to make the next step obvious.

If I can do that in my website, social media becomes easier, because the website carries the weight.

The biggest benefit: credibility you can control

When Nyakor said a website provides credibility, I did not fully understand it at first. I thought credibility came from likes, comments, and follower counts.

But credibility is deeper than popularity.

Credibility is what a serious buyer feels when they are deciding whether you are real, whether you are stable, whether you will deliver, and whether you are safe to do business with.

A good website signals credibility in quiet ways:

Consistency. Your logo, colors, tone, photography, and message match across pages.

Clarity. People understand what you offer within seconds.

Proof. Testimonials, photos, client results, press mentions, or examples of work.

Safety. Secure browsing, clear policies, clear payment steps, and no shady surprises.

Professionalism. Good writing, clean layout, working links, and fast loading.

Most people will not say, "This site feels credible." They will simply behave as if it is credible. They will read more. They will click. They will buy. They will contact you.

Or, if you ignore these details, they will leave quietly.

My turning point: I stopped building pages and started building paths

In my early attempts, I built pages like I was filling a folder.

Home page, about page, gallery, contact.

It looked complete, but it did not convert. It did not guide anyone. It was a collection of rooms with no hallway.

Nyakor helped me see the missing piece: the website is not a set of pages, it is a set of paths.

A visitor arrives with a question in their mind. Your job is to answer that question and guide them to the next right step.

So I started designing paths like this:

Path for the curious visitor. They arrive from social media. They want to understand me. I guide them to my story and my best work.

Path for the serious buyer. They arrive from search. They want a product. I guide them to the product page, proof, and checkout.

Path for the cautious buyer. They arrive from a recommendation. They want safety. I guide them to testimonials, policies, and contact details.

Path for the supporter. They like the mission but are not ready to buy. I guide them to subscribe to email, read key posts, and stay connected.

Once I started building paths, my website began to feel alive.

What makes a website "strong" in digital marketing terms

A strong website is not the prettiest website.

A strong website is the one that does its job.

Nyakor taught me to evaluate every page by asking: "What is this page *for*?"

Not what is it about, but what is it for.

A page can be for:

Attracting. It ranks in search, gets clicks, and pulls new people in.

Explaining. It makes your offer clear, removes confusion, and answers doubts.

Converting. It gets the visitor to take a step, buy, book, subscribe, or contact.

Retaining. It keeps people coming back through content, resources, and email.

If your site has pages that look nice but do none of these, you have decoration, not marketing.

And if your site does these well, it becomes your silent salesperson.

The essential pages I build first

When Nyakor and I talked about the "essential pages," the list was simple: About, Shop, Blog, Contact.

But what matters is not the page name. What matters is what that page achieves.

Here is how I think about these pages now, in plain, practical terms.

Home page

The home page answers:

Who is this for, what is offered, and what should I do next?

If the home page does not answer those fast, you lose people.

About page

The about page answers:

Why should I trust you, and why do you do this work?

I treat the about page as a credibility page, not a biography.

Offer page

This could be "Shop," "Services," "Work With Me," or "Book."

This page answers:

What exactly do I get, how much does it cost, and how do I buy it?

Blog or resources

This page answers:

Do you have depth, do you teach, do you prove expertise, do you show consistency?

The blog is also a search engine magnet if you write with discipline.

Contact page

This page answers:

How do I reach you, and what happens after I reach you?

If you make contact confusing, you lose business.

Trust and policy pages

People skip these until a problem happens, then they become very important. Also, buyers with money read them.

Examples:

Privacy policy, terms, refunds, shipping, and disclaimers.

You do not have to make them long. You have to make them clear.

The website as a story machine

In my studio, I tell stories with fabric, beadwork, texture, and color.

Online, I tell stories with words, images, layout, and structure.

The website is where those stories live in an organized way.

A social media caption is a shout.

A website page is a conversation.

That is why I love the blog, especially when it sits inside the website. In the book, we used a personal blog to share inspirations and stories behind the designs. That is not just "content." That is the brand becoming human.

A story-driven website does three things at once:

It attracts. Stories bring search traffic when people search for ideas, not only products.

It connects. People remember meaning more than marketing.

It sells without begging. When people understand the story, they buy with pride, not pressure.

If you sell a product without story, you compete on price.

If you sell a product with story, you compete on meaning.

The website as a conversion system

Some creators hear "conversion" and think of manipulation.

I do not.

I think of conversion as *helping someone complete a decision.*

Most visitors arrive confused. They like something, but they are unsure. They want to trust, but they need proof. They want to buy, but they need clarity.

A conversion system removes friction.

Friction is anything that makes the next step hard.

Examples of friction:

A page loads slowly.

A button is hard to find.

A product description is vague.

The buyer cannot tell what happens after checkout.

The contact form does not work.

There is no proof that anyone has bought before.

Nyakor kept repeating the basics: the storefront must be welcoming and easy to navigate, and it should be optimized so people can find it.

So I started treating every friction point like a loose thread. If you ignore a loose thread, the whole garment can unravel. If you fix it early, the work lasts.

Your website is where you build your list

I want to say this clearly, because it is one of the most profitable lessons in digital marketing.

If you do not build an email list, you are always starting over.

Likes do not belong to you. Followers do not belong to you. Reach does not belong to you.

But an email list is closer to ownership because you can reach people directly, without begging an algorithm.

In the book, the website opt-in form was used to grow a list and build stronger relationships. That is the point.

Your website should not only be a place to buy. It should be a place to join.

A visitor might not be ready to purchase today, but they might be ready to subscribe. If you capture that, you keep the relationship alive.

And once you have the relationship, you can serve them over time.

Search engines and the long game

The day I began to respect SEO, I began to respect patience.

Search is not a quick win. It is a long win.

When you build your website well, you set up small wins that compound. In the book, those wins were described as things like a feature, a backlink, a rise in organic visits, and how credibility grows over time through that compounding effect.

SEO pushes you toward quality, because the goal is not noise, it is usefulness.

But SEO only works if the website can carry it.

That means your site must be:

Fast.

Mobile-friendly.

Secure.

Structured.

In the book, Nyakor pushed for technical improvements like better loading speed, stronger mobile responsiveness, and structured metadata.

And the technical basics mattered: compressing images, caching, reducing unnecessary scripts, HTTPS, and a sitemap.

That is not "tech stuff." That is trust stuff.

A slow website is like a shop with a locked door.

A secure website is like a shop with proper lighting and a working lock.

People feel these things, even when they cannot explain them.

The website gives you a clean place to measure reality

Without measurement, digital marketing becomes emotion.

You feel like you are working hard, but you do not know what is working.

A website gives you clearer signals than social media, because you can track:

Which pages bring the most traffic.

Which sources bring the most buyers.

Which posts lead to email signups.

Which product pages get views but no purchases.

Where people drop off.

In the book, this mindset showed up as "data-driven growth," tracking traffic sources and performance so strategy can be refined.

Once I started treating analytics as truth, I stopped arguing with reality.

I could finally say, with evidence:

This page works.

This page confuses people.

This post brings buyers.

This platform brings attention but not sales.

And then I could adjust calmly, without drama.

How I build a website when I want it to produce results

I am going to speak from my own practice, as the teacher and guide, but I will keep it simple enough for anyone to apply.

I start with one promise

Not ten promises.

One.

If I cannot state my promise clearly, the website cannot either.

So I ask myself:

What do I help people do, or what do I help people get?

Then I say it in plain language.

I choose one primary action

A website that asks visitors to do five things usually gets them to do nothing.

So I choose one main action per page.

Examples:

Buy the hero product.

Book a consultation.

Subscribe to the list.

Read the guide.

I build the home page like a conversation

I imagine a visitor standing at my door.

They are not ready to hear my whole life story.

They want the short truth first.

So I answer, in order:

Who this is for.

What I offer.

Why it matters.

What to do next.

Proof.

More detail for those who want it.

I write product descriptions as if I am speaking to one person

Not like a catalog.

Not like a corporate brand.

One person.

I describe:

What it is.

Who it is for.

What problem it solves.

What makes it different.

What they receive.

How to buy.

I keep design clean and readable

I love beauty. I am a designer.

But online, beauty must serve clarity.

A page can look artistic and still be confusing.

So I prefer:

Strong contrast.

Big readable text.

Simple menus.

Clear buttons.

Enough spacing.

High-quality images that load fast.

I build trust on purpose

I include proof, policies, and contact clarity, because credibility does not happen by accident.

And I keep it honest.

A practical example from my world: turning "Kuel" into a website experience

When I named my collection "Kuel," I was not naming a product line only. I was naming a story.

That story needed a place to live.

So I imagined what a visitor should feel when they arrive on the site:

They should feel the star.

They should feel the heritage.

They should feel that the work is real, crafted, and grounded.

They should feel that buying is safe.

So I built the website around experiences:

A hero image that shows the craft, not only the final look.

A short brand statement that sets the tone.

A "Kuel Stories" section where the narrative is preserved and organized.

A shop that is not crowded, where each piece has room to breathe.

A clear contact path.

And most importantly, I treated the website as a place to return to, not a one-time launch.

That is the secret many people miss.

A website is not a launch event.

It is a living shop.

You sweep it.

You restock it.

You improve it.

You keep it open.

Key lessons I want you to carry from this chapter

I am going to leave you with the truths that changed my results.

A website is the center of your brand's digital life, not an accessory.

A website gives credibility because it shows stability, clarity, and seriousness.

A website must be welcoming, easy to navigate, and built so people can find it.

Technical strength is part of trust, speed, mobile, security, and structure.

SEO rewards patience and steady improvement, not panic.

And here is the simplest summary I can give you:

Social media can introduce you.

A website can keep you.

If you want digital marketing success that lasts, you do not build only where you can be removed. You build where you can stand.

That is why, in the next chapter, when we talk about brand identity, the website will remain the anchor. Because identity is not only what you say in posts. It is what people experience when they come home to your brand.

Chapter 5: Developing a Clear Brand Identity
The night I learned that a brand is not a logo

When Nyakor walked into my studio, she did not just see fabric and sketches. She saw a story that could travel. She asked what my designs meant, and I told her what I had never told the market in a clear way: my work was not "clothes." It was memory, heritage, and a message stitched into form. That was the first time I realized my problem was not talent. My problem was translation.

I had the craft. I had the meaning. But online, meaning does not magically appear. People do not "feel" your purpose just because you feel it. They need signals. They need a shape they can recognize, a voice they can trust, and repeated proof that you are who you say you are.

That is why Nyakor clapped her hands and said, "First, a logo. Something that embodies Kuel's essence."

At first, I resisted. I thought a logo was decoration. I thought branding was for big companies, not for someone who still had beads on the floor and unfinished hems on the table. But then she pulled one of my sketches, and we stared at it like it was a mirror. A stylized Nuer woman, adorned with beadwork, reaching for a star.

In that moment, Nyakor taught me a lesson I now teach you: **your brand identity is your story, made usable.**

A logo is a door sign. A brand identity is the house.

We spent hours brainstorming, refining, debating colors, and searching for a look that felt true to the name I chose, **Kuel**, the Nuer word for "star." That night, I did not just pick a logo. I began to build a language for my work.

This chapter is about building that language for your work, whether you sell fashion, consulting, music, books, soap, courses, art, or a service.

What "brand identity" really means

Brand identity is the set of choices that makes people recognize you, remember you, and trust you. It is what you repeatedly show and repeatedly say, so the market stops guessing who you are.

Brand identity includes:

- **Your promise:** what people can expect from you, every time.
- **Your positioning:** who you serve, what you solve, and what makes your way different.
- **Your personality and voice:** how you sound, how you behave, how you treat people.
- **Your visuals:** logo, color, typography, imagery style, layout habits.
- **Your experience:** how it feels to buy from you, read you, follow you, or work with you.

Many people think brand identity is "looking nice." That is too shallow. Looking nice is helpful, but it is not the real job.

The real job is this: **reduce confusion.**

If people are confused, they do not buy. If they do not remember you, they do not return. If you do not feel consistent, they do not trust you.

I will make it practical:

- When your visuals are random, people assume your business is random.
- When your message is vague, people assume your value is vague.
- When your tone changes every week, people assume you are performing, not serving.
- When your offer is unclear, people assume the risk is high.

A clear brand identity lowers perceived risk and raises belief.

Why brand identity matters more online than offline

Offline, you can rely on location, foot traffic, human warmth, and social proof in the room. Online, your visitor is one click away from leaving. They are not rude. They are busy.

So online, your brand identity has to do heavy work quickly:

- It has to answer, fast: **"Who is this for?"**
- It has to answer, fast: **"What do they do?"**
- It has to answer, fast: **"Why should I trust them?"**
- It has to answer, fast: **"Is this worth my time or money?"**

Nyakor once told me that my website had to become a "home" for my brand, a place where people do not just see products but experience the meaning behind them. That is branding in action. Not hype. Not shouting. **A home.**

A home has patterns:

- You recognize the door.
- You understand the rules.
- You feel safe inside.
- You can find what you need.
- You can recommend it to someone else without embarrassment.

That is what brand identity does in digital marketing.

The three layers of brand identity I use

When I teach brand identity, I separate it into three layers, because most people try to do everything at once and then quit.

Layer 1: Meaning

This is the heart.

- Why do you exist?
- What do you refuse to compromise?
- What change do you want to bring?
- What do you believe?

If you skip meaning, you will copy other brands, and your audience will feel it.

Layer 2: Message

This is the mouth.

- What do you say in one sentence?
- What do you repeat until people associate it with you?
- What words do you use often?
- What words do you never use?

If you skip message, your audience will like you but not know what to do next.

Layer 3: Look

This is the face.

- What colors do you own?
- What typography do you repeat?
- What style of images do you use?
- What does your logo represent?

If you skip look, your audience will struggle to recognize you, even if your work is good.

A strong identity needs all three, but you build them in order: **Meaning, then Message, then Look.**

Building your brand identity the way Nyakor made me do it

Nyakor did not let me chase beauty first. She forced me to answer hard questions.

I will give you the same path, as if you are sitting across from me in the studio.

Your Brand Identity Page (one page, no excuses)

Open a blank page. Title it: **"My Brand Identity."**

Then write the following sections.

1) My audience

Write a clear sentence:

- "I serve _____ who want _____ but struggle with _____."

Be honest. Do not try to serve "everyone." Serving everyone is the fastest way to sound like nobody.

2) My offer

Write a clear sentence:

- "I help them by providing _____ so they can achieve _____."

This keeps your marketing from turning into noise.

3) My difference

Write a clear sentence:

- "People choose me because _____."

This is not about ego. It is about clarity.

Your difference can be:

- lived experience
- speed
- quality
- cultural depth
- specialized skill
- ethical sourcing
- a specific method
- a specific style
- a specific promise you keep better than others

In my case, Kuel was not "another fashion brand." It was culture carried with respect.

4) My promise

Write a clear sentence:

- "Every time someone meets my brand, they will feel _____ and receive _____."

This becomes the standard for your content, your product, your service, your replies, your packaging, your emails.

5) My values

Pick 3 to 5. Define each in your own words.

Values are not posters. Values are rules.

Example:

- If you say "quality," what does that mean in practice?
- If you say "integrity," what will you refuse to do even if it pays?

- If you say "community," what do you do for the customer after the sale?

6) My personality

Choose 3 adjectives that describe how your brand behaves.

Examples:

- warm
- direct
- bold
- calm
- playful
- serious
- premium
- friendly
- scholarly
- rugged
- elegant

This matters because your personality shapes your tone, your photos, your design choices, and even the rhythm of your captions.

7) My story

Write 6 to 10 sentences.

Not a biography.

A story that explains:

- where you started
- what you saw
- what you decided to do
- who you do it for
- what you want people to experience

Nyakor pushed me to share my stories, not hide them, because people connect with the journey as much as the final product.

That is not a motivational quote. It is a marketing truth.

Turning meaning into a message people can repeat

A brand is strong when customers can describe it without effort.

If your customer cannot explain you, they cannot refer you.

So I build messaging in a way that forces simplicity.

Your one-line identity

Write:

- "I am the _____ for _____ who want _____."

Examples:

- "I am the writing coach for busy professionals who want a clear voice."
- "I am the ethical fashion studio for people who want culture without exploitation."
- "I am the home bakery for families who want simple, honest treats."

Your short pitch

Write 3 sentences:

- Sentence 1: who you serve and what you do
- Sentence 2: what makes you different
- Sentence 3: what to do next

Example (fashion):

"I design clothing rooted in heritage and made with care. Every piece carries a story and supports real artisans. If you want to wear something meaningful, start with the Kuel Stories collection."

Your tagline

A tagline is not a poem. It is a handle.

Good taglines are:

- short
- clear
- memorable
- consistent with your promise

Tagline patterns that work:

- "_____ made _____."
- "Where _____ meets _____."
- "For _____ who _____."
- "Wear _____. Live _____."
- "From _____ to _____."

If you cannot write a tagline yet, do not force it. Use your one-line identity until the tagline becomes obvious.

Your brand vocabulary

This part is quiet but powerful.

Pick:

- 10 words you want to be known for
- 10 words you will avoid

For Kuel, words like "heritage," "story," "artisan," "star," and "ethical" became pillars. (Your words will be different.)

This helps you stay consistent across:

- product descriptions
- captions
- email subject lines
- homepage copy
- ad headlines
- video scripts

Without vocabulary rules, your brand voice becomes a different person every week.

Designing a visual identity that is usable, not just pretty

Now we move to the part most people rush: visuals.

Nyakor loved aesthetics, but she wanted **function**. She wanted the identity to work on a phone screen, on a billboard, on a small icon, and inside an email header.

Remember the moment she said "First, a logo"? She did not mean "first, a decoration." She meant "first, a symbol we can build around."

Your logo: choose meaning over trends

A logo should be:

- recognizable at small sizes
- readable in one color
- connected to your meaning
- simple enough to repeat everywhere

If your logo is too detailed, it dies on a profile picture.

If your logo has no meaning, it becomes replaceable.

When I pulled out the sketch of the woman reaching for a star, it was not random art. It was my identity: heritage reaching forward.

Your logo does not have to be cultural like mine, but it must be honest.

Your colors: choose a small set you can own

Pick:

- 1 primary color
- 1 secondary color
- 1 accent color
- 2 neutral colors

That is enough.

When brands use 12 colors, they do not look "creative." They look undecided.

Color choices should match your personality:

- bold brands often use high contrast
- calm brands often use softer tones
- premium brands often use restrained palettes
- playful brands often use brighter accents

If you sell serious services, avoid colors that feel childish.

If you sell joyful products, avoid colors that feel like a funeral.

Your typography: pick one main font and one helper

Most brand confusion comes from typography chaos.

Choose:

- a headline font

- a body font

Then repeat them everywhere:

- website
- posts
- PDFs
- proposals
- pitch decks
- thumbnails

If you change fonts constantly, your content feels like it comes from different companies.

Your image style: decide your "camera behavior"

People underestimate this.

Make decisions like:

- Do we use bright, airy photos or dark, moody ones?
- Do we use studio backgrounds or real-life locations?
- Do we show faces often, or focus on product details?
- Do we use natural light or controlled lighting?
- Do we use sharp, clean edits or warm film-like tones?

Your image style is part of your identity. It signals quality, mood, and intent.

Your layout habits: repeat a few patterns

This is what makes your Instagram grid look "designed" without extra work.

Decide:

- where your logo sits on graphics
- how much white space you prefer

- whether titles are centered or left-aligned
- your usual border style (if any)
- your usual icon style (if any)

These are small decisions, but repeated decisions create recognition.

The "identity test" I use before I publish anything

Before I post, I ask myself five questions. You can use the same test.

Recognition

If someone sees this for one second, will they know it is me?

Clarity

If someone reads this, will they know what I do?

Consistency

Does this match my promise and personality?

Trust

Does this feel honest, or does it feel like I am trying to impress?

Action

Is the next step obvious?

If one answer is "no," I revise before I publish.

This is how you protect your brand without becoming perfectionist.

Brand identity is also behavior

A lot of people build pretty brand kits and then behave in a way that ruins trust.

Your identity is not only design. It is your actions.

If you claim "premium" but you reply late, you are not premium.

If you claim "warm" but you speak like a robot, you are not warm.

If you claim "ethical" but you hide your sourcing, you are not ethical.

In the Kuel journey, when pressure came from fast-fashion giants offering money, the brand identity had to stand firm. Identity is tested when it costs you something.

So I teach this: **build an identity you can afford to keep.**

Do not promise what you cannot deliver.

Do not borrow a personality you cannot live.

Do not copy a tone that does not fit your real voice.

A practical example: building Kuel's identity from the ground up

Let me show you how I would translate Kuel into a clean identity system, using the same decisions Nyakor and I made in the studio.

Meaning

- **Purpose:** preserve and share heritage through design
- **Promise:** every piece carries story and respect
- **Values:** craftsmanship, dignity, honesty, cultural pride, fair partnership

Message

- **One-line identity:** "Kuel is a star-driven fashion house carrying heritage into modern life."
- **Core themes:** story, star, artisan, legacy, ethical making
- **Tone:** warm, confident, respectful, direct

Look

- **Logo:** the woman reaching for a star
- **Color direction:** deep night tones (sky), warm gold accents (stars), earth neutrals (heritage)
- **Typography direction:** elegant serif for heritage, clean sans-serif for modern readability
- **Image style:** hands, beadwork, fabric texture, real artisans, cultural symbols used with care

Notice what is happening. Every piece matches the name "star." Nothing is random.

That is what you want.

A brand identity should feel like a single mind made it.

Common mistakes that destroy brand identity

I have made some of these mistakes myself, so I am not throwing stones. I am giving warnings.

Copying a brand you admire

Admiration is good. Copying is weak.

Borrow inspiration, but keep your own story.

Trying to look "big" before being clear

A polished site with vague messaging still fails.

Clarity first. Shine later.

Changing your identity every month

Consistency is not prison. It is trust.

If you change your colors every week, you reset recognition every week.

Over-designing

A brand kit that takes you 3 hours to make one post is a trap.

Your identity must be usable on tired days.

Being too clever

Clever headlines impress writers. Clear headlines convert customers.

Hiding behind general words

Words like "quality" and "excellence" mean nothing unless you prove them.

Show proof:

- photos
- process
- standards
- testimonials
- guarantees
- behind-the-scenes

Your Brand Kit (what to keep in one folder)

This is the operational side. Nyakor would love this part.

Create a folder called:

Brand Kit

Inside, keep:

- logo files (color, black, white)
- your color hex codes
- font names (and links for your own use)
- 10 photo examples that match your style
- your one-line identity and short pitch
- your tagline (if you have one)
- your "about" paragraph
- your vocabulary list (words you use, words you avoid)
- 3 to 5 post templates (simple ones)

This folder saves you from random marketing.

When you feel stuck, you do not "think." You pick from your kit and execute.

A short studio exercise (do it today)

If you do only one thing after reading this chapter, do this:

Write your one-line identity and put it in three places:

- your website homepage headline
- your social media bio
- your email signature (or profile)

Then publish one piece of content that proves it.

Proof can be:

- a behind-the-scenes photo
- a short story about why you started
- a product story

- a client result
- a process explanation

Remember what Nyakor told me: "You stand out by being yourself." That statement is branding, but only if you translate it into repeated signals.

Closing: the moment a brand becomes real

When Nyakor and I finally settled on the logo, I felt something shift in me. It was not only relief. It was ownership. I was no longer hiding behind my work, hoping the world would somehow understand it. I was choosing how the world would meet it.

Nyakor grinned and said, "Now, we build the world around it."

That sentence is the heart of brand identity.

You build the world around your work so your work can travel without losing its meaning.

And if you do this well, something beautiful happens.

People do not just buy.

They remember.

They return.

They tell others.

They become part of what you are building.

In the next chapter, we will go deeper into being found online, because your identity is not only about being seen, it is also about being searchable. The star needs a sky, but it also needs a map.

(Past chat)(Past chat)(Past chat)(Past chat)

Chapter 6: Search Engine Optimization (SEO)

I learned the hard way that a website can be beautiful and still be invisible.

I can build a clean homepage. I can write a strong "About" page. I can even publish blog posts that make people feel something. But if search engines cannot understand what I built, or if they cannot trust it, my work sits in the dark like a shop on a quiet street with no signboard.

That is what SEO fixes.

SEO is not magic. It is not "tricking Google." It is the disciplined work of making your website easy to discover, easy to understand, and worth recommending. In Google's own words, SEO is about helping search engines understand your content and helping users decide whether your site is what they want. (Google for Developers)

In this chapter, I will teach you SEO the way I would teach a younger version of myself: patiently, practically, and without making it sound like a secret society. I will also use my running example of my craft business and my conversations with Nyakor, not because the details must match your life, but because stories make the lessons stick.

1) What SEO really is (and what it is not)

When people hear "SEO," they often imagine one of two extremes:

- A mysterious algorithm that only insiders understand.
- A quick hack that pushes a page to the top overnight.

Both ideas create disappointment.

Here is the truth I want you to carry: **SEO is a long game built on clarity and trust.** It rewards websites that consistently help real people.

Google's SEO starter guide also makes a point I agree with deeply: there are no "secrets" that automatically put you first, and not every suggestion applies to every business. The goal is to make it easier for search engines to crawl, index, and understand your pages. (Google for Developers)

So SEO is not a single trick. It is a set of habits that turn your website into something search engines can recommend without embarrassment.

2) Start where most people skip: eligibility and trust

Before you chase rankings, make sure you are eligible to show up at all.

Google groups the basics into **Search Essentials**: technical requirements, spam policies, and key best practices. (Google for Developers)

Two points from that document matter for every beginner:

A) It does not cost money to appear in Google Search

If someone tells you they have a "special connection" to get you indexed for a fee, treat it like a scam. Google is clear that it does not cost money to appear in Search results. (Google for Developers)

B) Spam tactics can bury you

Google also publishes detailed spam policies and they are not theoretical. They cover things like hidden text, link abuse, and scaled content created mainly to manipulate rankings. ([Google for Developers](#))

Let me say this plainly: **if your strategy requires deception, you are building on sand.**

Nyakor once told me something that sounded harsh at the time, but saved me later:

"Panyim, never build a business on a method you would be ashamed to explain to your customers."

SEO is exactly that. You are building something you can explain with pride.

3) How search works in simple human language

Search engines do three big jobs:

Crawl

They discover pages by following links and reading sitemaps.

Index

They store and organize what they find so they can retrieve it fast.

Rank

They choose what to show first based on relevance, usefulness, and signals of trust.

You do not control those systems. You influence them.

Your job is to make every step easy:

- Make your pages accessible.
- Make your meaning clear.

- Make your site fast and usable.
- Make your content worth linking to.

That is the SEO mindset.

4) Keywords are not "stuffing," they are listening

The first time I heard "keywords," I thought it meant repeating the same phrase until the page looked ridiculous.

Nyakor corrected me with a better picture: **keywords are the words people use when they ask for help.**

In the manuscript, I describe SEO as making the website visible and treating search engines like treasure hunters scanning the web, while I create a clear path for them to follow.

That "clear path" begins with understanding what people type.

The manuscript recommends starting by identifying the words and phrases potential customers might search, using tools like Google Keyword Planner or Ubersuggest.

I will expand that into a practical method you can repeat.

A) Build your "seed list"

Start with 10–30 simple phrases that describe:

- What you sell
- Who you serve
- Where yoblems you solve

If I sell handcrafted wooden toys, my seeds might be:

- wooden toys for toddlers
- handmade wooden puzzles
- Montessori wooden toys

- educational wooden toys
- non-toxic wooden toys

If you run a cliin Juba

- maternal health services
- child immunization schedule
- affordable lab test near me

Your job is not to be clever. Your job is to be accurate.

B) Expand the list with tools and real-life language

Use keyword tools, yes. But also use:

- Your customer questions on WhatsApp
- Your Facebook comments
- Your own search history
- "People also ask" boxes on Google
- Related searches at the bottom of results

When you do this, you stop guessing and start listening.

C) Match keywords to intent

Every search has a goal. Usually it is one of these:

- **Know**: "what is…" "how to…" "why does…"
- **Do**: "buy…" "download…" "book appointment…"
- **Go**: "near me" "in [city]" "directions"

If the intent is "know," write a helpful article. If the intent is "do," build a clear service page or product page. If the intent is "go," you need local SEO signals.

This is where many sites fail. They write one type of page for every search and then wonder why it does not rank.

5) The foundation: if your website is weak, SEO collapses

In the manuscript, the "foundation" is described in simple terms: the site must be easy to navigate, mobile-friendly, and fast-loading.

That is correct, and it is more serious than people think.

Search engines want to recommend results that do not frustrate users. Users leave slow sites quickly. And when users leave quickly, it sends a bad signal.

Here is what I focus on before anything else.

A) Navigation that makes sense

Your menu should reflect how your customers think, not how you think.

A small business site can often survive with:

- Home
- Shop / S Resources
- Contact

If you have 17 menu items, you are not being "complete." You are being confusing.

B) Mobile friendliness

Most of my readers and customers, especially in African markets, browse on phones. A site that only looks good on a laptop is a luxury brochure, not a working business asset.

C) Speed

Speed is not a vanity metric. It is a sales metric.

Google's Core Web Vitals are part of how they measure page experience. They highlight three key metrics: LCP (loading), INP (responsiveness), and CLS (visual stability), with target thresholds such as LCP within 2.5 seconds, INP under 200 ms, and CLS under 0.1. (Google for Developers)

Even if you do not love technical details, respect what they mean:

- A page should load quickly.
- It should respond quickly when someone taps.
- It should not jump around while loading.

D) Security and basic technical hygiene

In the manuscript, I mention HTTPS and an XML sitemap as part of technical SEO improvements.

This is not optional anymore. HTTPS is baseline trust. A sitemap helps discovery, especially for new sites.

6) On-page SEO: make each page speak clearly

On-page SEO is the practice of making each page understandable at a glance.

The manuscript lists several key elements:

- **Title tags and meta descriptions**
- **Headings (H1, H2, H3)**
- **Internal linking**
- **Image optimization (filenames and alt text)**

Let me teach these like I build a physical product: one piece at a tim title tag is often the first impression in search results. It should:

- Tell the truth about the page
- Include the main keyword naturally
- Make someone want to click

Bad: **Home**
Better: **Handcrafted Wooden Toys for Toddlers | Wonders of Wood**

I always ask myself: *If this title was the only thing someone saw, would they know what I offer?*

B) Meta descriptions

Meta descriptions do not always "rank" you, but theyite meta descriptions like a short invitation:

- Who it is for
- What it solves
- What to expect

Example:

Discover safe, handcrafted wooden toys designed for toddlers. Browse puzzles, animal sets, and gift-ready pieces made with care.

C) Headings that organize thought

Headings are not decoration. They are structure.

Use one H1 per page. Use H2s for main sections, H3s for smaller sections.

If your page is a wall of text, many readers will not even try. Search engines also use structure to understand what matters.

D) Internal links

Internal links are your own roads.

They help:

- Users find what they need
- Search engines discover more pages
- Important pages gain strength

In the manuscript, internal linking is framed as guiding visitors to other relevant pages.

That is the exact mindset: **guide, do not trap.**

A blog post about "Montessori play" should link to your Montessori product collection. A service page should link to FAQs. A clinic page should link to appointment booking and operating hours.

E) Image optimization

Images can bring traffic through image search, and they also support accessibility.

The manuscript highlights descriptive filenames and alt text.

I do this:

- Filename: `wooden-giraffe-puzzle-toddler.jpg`
- Alt text: "Handcrr toddlers"

Not poetry. Not marketing. Just accurate description.

7) Content: the bridge between you and the searcher

In the manuscript, content is described as "the bridge between your website and potential customers," and the advice is to publish useful material like tutorials, behind-the-scenes posts, and customer stories.

This is where SEO becomes human.

Search engines ansity." They are trying to find pages that satisfy a need. And needs are human.

So I build content around real questions.

A) The three content types that win in SEO

If you are new, focus on these:

Evergreen guides
"How to choose a wooden toy for a 2-year-old"
"Beginner guide to remote work taxes"
"What to expect at your first prenatal visit"

Problem-solvers
"Why your website is slow and how to fix it"
"Why your Facebook re*Trust builders**
Your story, your process, your values, your proof.

In the manuscript, the "About" page is described as a place to tell your story because people connect with authentic narratives.

That is not "branding talk." That is conversion psychology.

B) Write for the reader first, and you will usually please Google too

Google's SEO guide says the website is built with users in mind, and that one of those users is a search engine. ([Google for Developers](#))

That sentence is worth remembering. You are not writing for robots. You are making meaning clear enough that both humans and machines can understand.

8) Technical SEO: the unseen hero

Some people treat technical SEO as "developer stuff." I disagree., you need to understand the basics so you can ask the right questions and avoid being misled.

The manuscript calls technical SEO "the unseen hero" and lists practical actions like compressing images, leveraging caching, minimizing scripts, improving mobile experience, using HTTPS, and creating an XML sitemap.

Let me translate that into a simple set of priorities.

A) Crawlability

- Make sure important pages are not blocked.
- Have a clean sitemap.
- Avoid accidental duplicate pages.

Google's SEO guide also discusses duplicate content and canonical URLs, reminding site owners that multiple URLs showing the same content can waste crawling resources and confuse users. (Google for Developers)

B) Site speed and stability

Use Google's Core Web Vitals targets as your compass. (Google for Developers)

You do not need perfection. You need progress.

C) Mobile usability

Test your pages on a cheap phone, not only on your own devi using older phones with slow networks.

D) Clean URL structure

A URL should tell a story:

Good: `/wooden-toys/montessori-puzzles/`
Bad: `/product?id=12345&ref=abc`

9) Structured data: help search engines label what you built

Structured data is not mandatory, but it can help search engines interpret your page and sometimes qualify you for rich results.

Google explains structured data as markup that helps them understand the content of a page and display richer search features in some cases. (Google for Developers)

If you use WordPress, many SEO plugins can help here, but do not treat plugins like miracles. Treat them like tools you must still inspect.

10) Backlinks: building bridges, not begging for votes

Backlinks are one of the most misunderstood parts of SEO.

The manuscript introduces backlinks as "votes of confidence," and then immediately corrects the wrong instinct: do not beg or buy links, provide value so people have a reason to showcase your work.

That is the right principle.

Backlinks are not just about rankings. They are about relationships and reputation.

Here are backlink methods I actually respect:

A) Get featured where your audience already trusts

If you sell toys, parenting blogs and education sites make sense. The manuscript gives exactly these examples as categories to pursue.

If you run a local service, local news and community sites can be powerful.

B) Write guest posts that teach

Not spam. Real teaching.

C) Create link-worthy assets

Examples:

- A free checklist
- A simple calculator
- A resource list
- A data-backed local guide

When you create something useful, people cite it naturally.

D) Reviews and local citations

If you serve a place, reviews matter. They also build trust beyond search engines.

11) Measurement: SEO without tracking is just hope

The manuscript reminds us tnds using tools like Google Analytics to track which keywords and strategies drive traffic, then adjust.

I agree, and I go one step further:

I track the right things, not everything.

Here is what I watch weekly:

- Total organic clicks (from Search Console)
- Top pages gaining clicks
- Queries bringing impressions but es)
- Pages that lost clicks (often competition or relevance)
- Conversion actions (email sign-ups, purchases, calls)

And I use tracking to choose my next move, not to panic.

12) Patience: the part nobody wants, but everybody needs

This section matters enough that I want to slow down.

In the manuscript, I describe the moment I realized SEO is not instant gratification. It requires consistency and long-term thinking.

I have lived that.

There is also a description of what SEO experts call the "sandbox effect," a waiting period before new sites rank competitively.

Whether you call it a sandbox or simply "trust same:

Search engines reward history.

You are not only building pages. You are building signals over time:

- People clicking and staying
- Other sites linking to you
- Your site staying consistent
- Your content staying helpful

The manuscript captures this compounding effect: small wins like an article feature or a backlink can stack over time, building credibility and visibility.

That is the heart of organic growth.

13) My weekly SEO rhythm (a system you can repeat)

I do not treat SEO like a one-time project. I treat it like maintenance of a working machine.

Here is a weekly rhythm that works even with limited time:

**WeSearch Console: what gained, what dropped

- Improve one page that already has impressions
- Publish or update one helpful piece of content
- Add intern the new one

Monthly (half day)

- Run a speed check and fix obvious issues
- Check for broken links
- Refresh top-performing pages with updated sections
- Do outreach for one partnership or feature

Quarterly (1 day)

- Review site structure
- Identify content gaps
- Consolidate overlapping articles (to avoid internal competition)
- Plan the next 90 days of content

This rhythm is simple, but it turns SEO into a steady practice instead of random burss that quietly destroy good work**

I have made some of these mistakes myself, so I am not preaching.

A) Writing content for algorithms, not people

If your page reads like a robot wrote it, people leave. If people leave, you lose.

B) Publishing lots of pages with little value

Google's spam policies explicitly warn against scaled content abuse, which is mass-producing pages mainly to manipulate rankings. (Google for Developers)

Quality beats volume, especially for small teams.

C) Hidden tricks

Hidden text and link abuse are specifically called out as spam. (Google for Developers)

If you are hiding something from users but showing it to search engines, you are walking toward trouble.

D) Ignoring user experience

If the site is slow, jumpy, or hard to use, people will not stay. Core Web Vitals exists for a reason. (Google for Developers)

15) The SEO promise: your work becomes discoverable while you sleep

When I rely only on paid ads, my visibility stops when my money stops.

When I build SEO, something different happens.

My pages keep working even when I am away. They keep answering questions. They keep sending people to my shop, my services, my ideas.

In the manuscript, the metaphor is simple: building an online presence is like creating a treasure map, and with the right keywords, content, and optimizations, people can discover what you built.

That is still my favorite way to say it.

A good website is not just a shop. It is a guide.

A good SEO strategy is not just ranking. It is **being findable when someone needs you.**

So I will end this chapter with the same invitation I give myself when I feel tired or impatient:

Build the path. Keep the path clear. Keep walking.

Chapter 7: The Power of Social Media Marketing

I used to think social media was noise.

A place where people talk too much, show too much, and forget too quickly.

Then I watched a single comment change the direction of a brand.

It happened in a quiet room. A desk. A phone. A blank page waiting for the first post. In the book's earlier scenes, I am in my studio with Nyakor, trying to figure out how to be seen. She calls social media a megaphone, and she pushes me toward visual platforms where storytelling and craft can be felt, not just explained.

That same lesson shows up again in a different setting: a workshop, a new Instagram page, and an uncle who doubts the whole idea. The first real sign of life is not a sale. It is a message from a stranger, a question, and a chance to respond like a human being.

That is where social media starts.

Not with "marketing."

With **contact**.

With a person on the other side.

Social Media Is Not a Billboard

A billboard talks. A conversation listens.

When I asked Nyakor how I could engage an audience I could not see, she did not tell me to post more. She told me to **listen first**, to read what people write, and to treat social media like a two-way exchange.

That sentence sounds simple, but it changes everything.

Because once you accept that social media is a conversation, you stop chasing vanity numbers and start building trust. Likes are fine, but the real signal is when people:

- ask questions
- share your post with someone else
- save it for later
- reply with their own story
- argue with you and stay in the room

That is not "traffic." That is relationship.

In the workshop story, the turning point is the realization that social media is not only for selling. It becomes a community where people want to engage, learn, and belong.

When you build your social media around that truth, you stop sounding like an advertiser. You start sounding like a person who has something real to offer.

Choosing Platforms Like a Strategist, Not Like a Tourist

Most people choose platforms the way they choose music. Whatever is popular, whatever is loud, whatever their friends are using.

I choose platforms the way I choose tools in my studio: by function.

Nyakor and I focus on platforms that fit visual storytelling and product demonstration. In the fashion example, we decide to lean into Instagram, Pinterest, and TikTok because visuals carry the message before the caption even starts.

Here is how I think about platforms when I'm teaching someone who is starting from zero:

Instagram

Good for:

- behind-the-scenes
- short videos
- brand personality
- community replies and DMs

Watch out for:

- posting without a "series" idea
- relying only on polished photos
- ignoring comments

TikTok

Good for:

- quick education
- product demos
- storytime clips
- strong reach when you find a repeatable format

Watch out for:

- trying to be funny when your brand is serious
- making random posts without a theme

Pinterest

Good for:

- search-based discovery
- long shelf life
- getting clicks to your website or blog

Watch out for:

- treating it like Instagram
- posting without clear keywords and pin titles

Facebook

Good for:

- groups
- older demographics
- community discussion and local reach

Watch out for:

- mixing personal drama with brand work
- posting like a newspaper headline without a reason to comment

LinkedIn

Good for:

- B2B services
- professional proof and credibility
- partnerships and speaking opportunities

Watch out for:

- copying Twitter-style posts that say nothing
- writing like a corporate memo

YouTube

Good for:

- deep teaching
- authority building
- evergreen content

Watch out for:

- perfectionism that delays publishing for months

You do not need to be everywhere.

You need to be **where your people already are**, and you need to show up with a clear reason.

Your First Job Is Not Posting, It Is Becoming Recognizable

Recognition is not fame.

Recognition is when your content feels consistent enough that someone can see it and say, "This is you."

Nyakor told me that authenticity is the key, and she pushed me to share my process, my late nights, my breakthroughs, and the reasons behind my work, not only the finished product.

That is how a person becomes a brand without becoming fake.

So, I teach social media in layers:

Layer One: The "Voice"

Your voice is how you sound when you are calm and honest.

If you try to write like someone else, the audience feels it. They might not say it, but they sense it. And when people sense performance, they hesitate to trust.

Your voice should carry:

- your values
- your humor (if you have it)
- your seriousness (if that is your nature)
- your way of teaching and telling stories

Layer Two: The "Signature"

A signature is a repeatable pattern that becomes yours.

Examples:

- every Monday you post a short lesson
- every Wednesday you post behind-the-scenes
- every Friday you answer one common question
- every weekend you share a customer story

People love patterns because patterns reduce effort. They know what they will get from you.

Layer Three: The "Series"

A series is when you pick one message and teach it across many posts, from different angles.

A fashion brand series might be:

- fabric selection stories
- sketch-to-stitch videos
- "why this design exists" mini-talks

A service brand series might be:

- common mistakes
- quick fixes
- before-and-after case studies

A product brand series might be:

- how it is made
- how to use it
- customer proof

This is how you make social media less stressful. You stop inventing ideas daily. You start working from a stable set of themes.

Engagement Is a Skill, Not a Personality Trait

Some people think engagement is for extroverts.

That is false.

Engagement is not about being loud. It is about being present.

In the story, I move from speaking into the void to building a real community by replying, asking questions, and treating every interaction like it matters.

And there are rules that work across every niche.

The book lists "Golden Rules of Engagement," and I keep them on my wall because they are basic and powerful: respond quickly, be genuine, and invite further conversation by asking questions.

I want to translate that into real practice.

How I Reply Without Sounding Like a Robot

When someone comments, I do not reply with "Thanks!"

I reply with:

- their name (if it's visible)
- one specific response to what they said
- one question to keep the talk going

Example:

"Thank you for asking. I use locally sourced materials, and I'm careful about quality. What age is your child, and what kind of play do they enjoy most?"

In the workshop story, the shift happens because replies are warm, informative, and human, and that warmth turns simple comments into trust.

What Engagement Really Builds

Engagement builds four things:

- **trust** (they believe you are real)
- **memory** (they remember you)
- **feedback** (you learn what people want)
- **distribution** (platforms push what people react to)

So yes, engagement can help reach.

But the deeper value is that engagement tells you what message is landing and what message is being ignored.

Content Strategy: Consistency Without Burnout

Consistency is not "posting every day until you hate your business."

Consistency is showing up often enough that people do not forget you.

In the book's social media teaching section, I learn that inconsistent posting makes people drift away, and I commit to posting regularly.

The book also gives a simple "Content Plan Basics" idea: post regularly, vary content types, and stay authentic by sharing real experiences, not only promotions.

Here is the version I teach inside my own work.

My "Three-Bucket" Content Plan

I create content in three buckets:

Bucket A: Proof

- finished work
- before/after
- testimonials
- results
- customer stories

Bucket B: Process

- behind-the-scenes
- how it's made
- daily routines
- tools and setups
- mistakes and fixes

Bucket C: Teaching

- tips
- myths to correct
- common questions
- short lessons
- simple guides

If I post only Proof, people feel sold to.

If I post only Process, people get bored.

If I post only Teaching, people may learn but not buy.

Three buckets balance the page.

Short-Form Content That Actually Works

The book highlights that short-form content like Stories and Reels is effective for engagement.

I agree, but I treat it like this:

- Stories are for daily contact
- Reels are for reach
- Posts are for identity
- Lives are for trust

And if you want a simple rhythm:

- Stories most days
- Reels a few times a week
- Posts a few times a week
- Live sessions when you have a reason

No hero schedule. Just a schedule you can live with.

Collaboration: Borrowed Trust Done the Right Way

Collaboration can be cheap or powerful.

Cheap collaboration is when you pay someone with followers to mention you once, then vanish.

Powerful collaboration is when you build with someone whose audience overlaps with yours, and you create content that serves both groups.

The book makes this point in two places: collaboration expands reach, and partnering with influencers and peers can bring new audiences and fresh energy.

Here is how I do it without wasting money.

My Rule for Influencers

I do not ask, "How many followers?"

I ask:

- do they speak to the people I want?
- do their followers reply, or do they only scroll?
- do they have credibility, or only popularity?
- do they create content that matches my values?

Micro-influencers often outperform big influencers because trust is closer.

My Rule for Partnerships

A partnership must have a clear deliverable:

- a joint live session
- a shared giveaway
- a mini-series where we both post
- a guest feature and a linked landing page
- a co-created product bundle

If there is no deliverable, the partnership is only a friendship, and friendships are fine, but they should not be called marketing.

Building a Community, Not Just an Audience

An audience claps.

A community talks back.

The book says this directly: engagement can become something more meaningful, and that "more" is community. People ask questions, share ideas, and even say your content pushed them to start their own project.

That is the real payoff of social media.

Because once you build community, you gain:

- free research (they tell you what they need)
- loyalty (they stay even when you miss a week)
- word-of-mouth (they bring their friends)
- protection (they defend you when someone attacks unfairly)

So I teach community-building as a practice:

Community Practices I Use

- I reply like I mean it.
- I remember repeat commenters.
- I ask questions that invite stories, not only yes/no answers.
- I run polls and let the results guide content ideas. (The workshop story shows how polls pull people into the brand's decisions.)
- I share small wins and thank people for being part of the road.

Community is not built by "growth hacks."

It is built by repeated respect.

Turning Social Attention Into Business Results

I want to be honest here.

Many people get stuck at likes.

They post. They grow a page. They get comments. They feel famous. They stay broke.

That happens when social media is separated from the rest of the business.

In earlier chapters, we build the website, brand identity, and SEO. Social media is the bridge that brings people into those assets.

So I teach social media as a path:

Attention → Trust → Action

Attention

Attention comes from:

- short videos
- shares
- search-based discovery (Pinterest, YouTube)
- collaborations

Trust

Trust comes from:

- consistent themes
- proof
- real replies and conversations
- showing the process, not only the result

Action

Action comes from:

- clear calls-to-action
- a landing page that matches the post
- an offer that solves a clear problem
- a way to contact you
- a way to buy

If your social page has no path, people get excited and then disappear.

So I create paths like:

- "Read the full guide on my site"
- "Join my email list for the checklist"
- "Book a call"
- "Shop the collection"
- "Download the free starter kit"

And I keep the path simple. One post, one main action.

Metrics That Matter, Without Becoming a Slave to Numbers

Numbers can teach you, or they can bully you.

The book lists what I watched after my early posts: engagement rate, active times, and follower growth, and it explains that tracking helps refine future posts.

That is exactly right.

I focus on a few practical metrics:

Engagement Rate

I watch it because it tells me whether I am connecting.

If reach is high and engagement is low, people are seeing but not caring.

That is a message: change the hook, change the message, change the visuals, or change the offer.

Saves and Shares

These are stronger than likes.

A like can be a reflex.

A save means value.

A share means trust.

Click-Through

If I want website traffic, I track clicks.

If clicks are low, I check:

- did I give a reason to click?
- does the link match the promise?
- did I place the call-to-action clearly?

Conversation Quality

This one is not a dashboard metric, but it matters.

Are people asking real questions?

Are they telling stories?

Are they repeating your language back to you?

That is brand formation happening in real time.

Handling Criticism, Low Posts, and the "Void" Feeling

Every creator meets the void.

You post and nothing happens.

You post and it flops.

You post and someone mocks you.

The book describes those moments clearly: posts that do not perform well, the feeling of speaking into emptiness, and the reminder that consistency and authenticity keep people engaged over time.

That is not theory. That is emotional reality.

Here is what I do:

I Don't Judge a Post in the First Hour

Some posts need time.

Some need shares.

Some need the right people to find them.

I Study Instead of Sulking

If a post flops, I ask:

- was the hook weak?
- was the message unclear?
- did I post at a bad time?
- did I use the wrong format?
- did I try to be someone I'm not?

I Keep My Identity Bigger Than a Metric

A number is not a verdict on your worth.

It is only a signal about a piece of content on one day.

I Use Criticism as Raw Material

The book also says I learned to handle criticism constructively and use negative feedback to improve content.

I agree, with a boundary:

- if criticism is about the work, learn from it
- if criticism is about your humanity, ignore it

Some people are not correcting you. They are just projecting their pain.

Staying Consistent While the Platforms Change

Trends change. Features change. People shift.

But the core stays the same.

The book's guidance is practical: monitor engagement with built-in tools, adjust based on data, experiment with content types, keep updating content, engage through comments and messages, run seasonal campaigns, and stay current with what is happening in digital marketing.

If you do those things, you will not panic every time a platform updates an algorithm.

Because your real edge will not be a trick.

Your real edge will be:

- consistency
- clarity
- relationship
- useful content
- a brand that people recognize

The First Post That Starts the Journey

I want to end this chapter the way the story ends: with the courage to post.

A first post is scary because it feels like standing in a public square with your heart in your hands.

But the book's "Final Thoughts" say it well: starting is intimidating, but big journeys start with a single step, and the world is full of people who want to connect and support.

So here is what I want you to do after reading this chapter:

A Simple Practice (No Perfection Required)

- choose one platform
- write one short post that tells a small truth about your work
- add one photo or video that shows the process
- ask one real question at the end
- reply to every comment like it matters

That is enough to begin.

Not with noise.

With contact.

With a person on the other side.

And when that first comment arrives, treat it like a visitor who entered your studio. Offer them warmth. Offer them clarity. Offer them respect.

That is how social media becomes power.

Chapter 9: A Cohesive Digital Marketing Strategy

I used to think digital marketing was a pile of separate tasks.

A website here. A few posts there. An ad when I had money. A blog when I had energy. A logo when I felt confident. Then I would wonder why my results felt random.

One week, people would love my posts. The next week, silence.

One month, my website would get traffic. The next month, it would feel like a ghost town.

I was working hard, but I was not moving with direction.

That is the moment I finally understood what a cohesive strategy means. It means every piece of your digital work supports the same promise, the same audience, and the same next step. It means your website, your content, your social media, your email, and even your paid ads are not competing with each other. They are cooperating.

When Nyakor and I started building my brand, the first thing we did was decide what story we were telling, and why anyone should care. Then we made the website our home base, not because social media is useless, but because a website gives credibility and a stable "home" for your brand.

After that, we stopped treating platforms like trophies. We chose platforms based on where my people already were, and how they liked to consume content.

Then we added structure, because passion without structure becomes inconsistency. We built a simple content calendar so the audience could trust my presence.

Then we measured what worked, adjusted, and kept going.

That, in plain language, is what a cohesive digital marketing strategy is.

Now I will teach you how I do it, in a way you can apply whether you sell fashion, books, coaching, services, or a small product made by your hands.

The problem most people have (and why you might feel stuck)

Most people do digital marketing like this:

They start with excitement.

They post when they feel inspired.

They try a new platform because someone said it is "hot."

They copy a tactic that worked for a bigger creator.

They run a paid ad because they are tired of waiting.

Then they burn out, because it feels like pushing a heavy cart on sand.

The issue is not intelligence. The issue is alignment.

A tactic is not a strategy.

A channel is not a strategy.

A post is not a strategy.

A strategy is a set of choices that creates focus.

The choices sound simple, but they decide everything:

- Who am I serving?
- What do I want them to believe about me?

- What do I want them to do next?
- Where will I meet them?
- What will I publish and how often?
- How will I know what is working?
- How will I improve without losing myself?

If you cannot answer those questions, your marketing becomes noise, even if you are talented.

A cohesive strategy turns noise into a path.

The "single thread" rule: one promise, one audience, one next step

When I think about cohesion, I think about sewing.

If you stitch a garment with random threads, it will tear.

If you stitch with one strong thread and you keep your pattern steady, the garment holds.

Your strategy needs a "single thread":

One promise.
What do you help people achieve, feel, or solve?

One audience.
Not everyone. A real group with a real problem.

One next step.
What do you want them to do after they discover you?

That next step matters more than your follower count.

You can have ten thousand followers who never take a step with you.

Or you can have two hundred people who trust you, and your life changes.

When Nyakor asked, "Where does your audience spend most of their time?" that question forced focus. Focus is the beginning of cohesion.

Step 1: Start with your story, not your tools

A cohesive strategy does not begin with tools. It begins with meaning.

If your story is unclear, everything you publish will sound like a sales pitch or a performance.

Your story answers:

- Why do I do this?
- What do I believe about this work?
- What makes my work different from a hundred others?
- What do I refuse to compromise?

In the book's original build, the first step was defining the brand story and the unique selling proposition, then making sure the brand personality reflects values and vision.

Here is how I teach it in my own voice.

My story worksheet (the one I actually use)

Origin moment:
What happened that made you start?

Enemy:
What problem are you fighting against? (confusion, poor quality, exploitation, laziness, isolation)

Promise:
What change do you help people reach?

Proof:
Why should they trust you? (skill, results, lived experience, process)

Voice:
How do you sound? (direct, warm, bold, calm)

Values:
What will you not trade away, even for money?

If you write this well, your website copy becomes easier.

Your posts become easier.

Your videos become easier.

Your emails become easier.

You stop guessing who you are each time you publish.

That is cohesion.

Step 2: Build your "home base" (your website) and give every platform a job

Social media is borrowed land. Your website is home.

You can grow on borrowed land, yes. But borrowed land can change rules overnight.

A website is not only a place to sell. It is a place to gather trust.

In the original text, my question was, "Do I really need a website when social media exists?" and the answer was yes, because the website is a digital storefront and adds credibility.

A cohesive strategy uses the website as the center, and every other platform has a job that supports it.

Give each channel a job (no channel should be confused)

- **Website:** trust, conversions, search traffic, detailed pages
- **Blog:** depth, SEO, long-term discovery, authority
- **Email:** retention, relationship, repeat attention
- **Instagram or TikTok:** reach, attention, human face, quick stories
- **YouTube or podcast:** depth, long-form trust, education
- **Pinterest:** discovery, evergreen clicks, visual search
- **Paid ads:** acceleration, controlled testing, retargeting

If you do not assign a job, you will waste energy.

You will post "everything everywhere," and you will still feel invisible.

Step 3: Choose platforms based on your people, not your ego

I learned this the hard way.

I used to spread myself thin. I wanted to be "everywhere."

Then Nyakor forced a better question: where are my ideal customers already spending time?

In the original content, we focused on Instagram, TikTok, and YouTube because the audience responded to visual storytelling.

That is not a rule for everyone. It is a method.

My platform selection filter

I choose a platform when:

- my audience is already active there

- my content style fits the platform (visual, writing, audio, teaching)
- I can publish consistently without hating my life
- the platform can push people toward my next step

I avoid a platform when:

- I only want it because others are succeeding on it
- I cannot commit to a basic schedule there
- I cannot tell my story properly there
- it will distract me from my home base

Cohesion means fewer platforms, better execution.

Step 4: Create a content calendar that matches your real life

I used to post in bursts.

Some weeks I would post daily, then disappear for a month.

The book names this as an early mistake, and it is one of the most common mistakes.

Consistency is not about perfection. It is about reliability.

In the original example, our weekly schedule looked like this: Monday behind-the-scenes, Wednesday styling tip, Friday customer story, Sunday live Q&A.

That is a strong pattern because it mixes:

- process
- education
- proof
- interaction

Here is how I expand that idea into a cohesive system you can copy.

My "four content pillars" approach

I always rotate these four types:

Process:
behind-the-scenes, how I work, what I am building

Proof:
results, testimonials, case studies, before/after, screenshots (when allowed)

Teaching:
short lessons, myths, simple steps, definitions, tools

Person:
my story, what I learned, why I believe what I believe, what I refuse to compromise

If your calendar includes all four, you will not sound like a salesperson, and you will not sound like a stranger. You will sound like a real builder.

A realistic publishing rhythm (for someone with limited time)

- one strong piece each week (blog post, video, or podcast)
- three to five short posts that reuse parts of that strong piece
- one email to your list, written from the week's main idea
- one day for review and planning

This is how you stay consistent without burnout.

Step 5: Make engagement a strategy, not a habit

Engagement is not "replying when you remember."

Engagement is how you build trust.

In the original section, it was clear: content was not enough, I had to interact, respond, ask for feedback, and share user content so people felt part of the journey.

Here is how I structure engagement so it supports the whole strategy.

The "three layers" of engagement

Layer one: quick replies
respond to comments, respond to DMs with short answers, thank people

Layer two: questions
ask what they want to see, what they struggle with, what they fear

Layer three: community rituals
weekly live session, monthly challenge, customer spotlight, behind-the-scenes day

You do not need a large following to do this.

You need consistency.

And yes, engagement should lead somewhere. That "somewhere" is your next step.

If your next step is an email list, then your engagement should often invite people into that list.

If your next step is a consultation, your engagement should invite a conversation.

If your next step is a product page, your engagement should educate people enough to feel ready.

Step 6: Build measurement into the plan, so you can adapt without panic

This is where many creators fail, not because they do not have data, but because they do not know what to do with it.

In the original text, after a few months, we saw some posts performed better, then analyzed engagement data and adjusted.

That is how real marketing works.

You do not guess forever.

You test, observe, adjust, and keep going.

The only numbers I track at first

I keep it simple:

- **Reach:** how many people saw it
- **Engagement:** did they react, comment, save, share
- **Clicks:** did they move toward my website or offer
- **Conversions:** did they subscribe, buy, book, download
- **Retention:** did they come back again

Then I ask:

- what topic got the strongest saves or shares?
- what format got the strongest watch time?
- what headline got clicks?
- what page converted?
- where do people drop off?

Cohesion means you track numbers that match your goal.

If your goal is email growth, likes alone do not matter.

If your goal is sales, reach alone does not matter.

Numbers must serve the mission, not the ego.

Step 7: Keep consistency, keep learning, keep shipping

A cohesive strategy is not a one-time setup. It is ongoing work.

The original text says it plainly: building an online brand is a continuous journey, and it lists actions like updating content, engaging through comments and messages, launching seasonal campaigns, and staying aware of trends.

I translate that into one sentence:

Keep showing up. Keep improving. Keep publishing.

That is why the phrase "It starts with a click" matters. Because the first action breaks fear.

Many people never click.

They plan forever.

They watch tutorials forever.

They keep polishing a brand that has never met the market.

A cohesive strategy does not wait for confidence. It builds confidence through action.

Putting it all together: the one-page strategy map I use

When Nyakor and I plan, we can write the whole strategy on one page.

I will show you my version.

One-page strategy map

Audience:
who I serve, what they want, what they struggle with

Promise:
the change I help them reach

Offer:
what I sell or provide (product, service, book, coaching, subscription)

Next step:
email list, purchase, consultation, download, follow

Home base:
website pages that matter (home, about, offer page, contact, blog)

Main channel:
the primary platform where I show up consistently

Support channel:
one extra platform that helps discovery

Content pillars:
process, proof, teaching, person

Publishing rhythm:
what I post weekly, and when

Measurement:
the few numbers that matter for this season

Review day:
weekly review, monthly review

If you can fill this page, you have cohesion.

If you cannot fill it, you are not ready for advanced tactics yet.

And that is good news, because it means you know what to fix.

A full example: how I would apply this for a new digital brand

Let me give you a clean example, using a simple brand.

Imagine I am launching a small coaching service for people who want to start a website.

The cohesive plan

Audience: new writers and small business owners who need online visibility
Promise: I help you launch a simple website that attracts real visitors
Offer: website setup plus a monthly support plan
Next step: free checklist download (email capture)
Home base pages: landing page, services page, blog, contact
Main channel: YouTube short lessons
Support channel: Pinterest pins pointing to blog posts
Content pillars:

- process: behind-the-scenes builds
- proof: before/after website screenshots
- teaching: short lessons on setup and SEO basics
- person: my story, my beliefs about honest work

Publishing rhythm:

- one video weekly (main piece)
- three short clips from that video
- one blog post that expands the lesson
- one email with a personal teaching note
- daily light engagement replies

Measurement:

- email signups per week
- clicks from social to website
- consult requests per month
- pages that convert best

That is cohesion. Everything supports the next step.

The common traps that break cohesion (and how I avoid them)
Trap: "More platforms will fix it"

No. Better messaging and better consistency fixes it.

Trap: "I need a new logo first"

No. You need clarity first. Design comes after clarity.

Trap: "I will start when I have better equipment"

No. Start with what you have. Improve as you go.

Trap: "I posted once and nothing happened"

Cohesion needs repetition. Trust grows through steady presence.

Trap: "I am doing everything right but it is slow"

Sometimes it is slow because you are early. That is normal. Keep tracking, keep improving, keep publishing.

My closing lesson for this chapter

A cohesive digital marketing strategy is not a secret trick.

It is disciplined alignment.

You define your story.
You build your home base.
You choose the right platforms.

You create a calendar and stay consistent.
You engage like a real human.
You measure and adjust using real data.
You keep showing up, because this is ongoing work.

If you do these things, you stop feeling like you are throwing stones into the dark.

You start building a path people can walk with you.

And if you are still hesitating, remember the line that helped me move: it starts with a click.

Final Note

When I started writing this book, I was trying to solve a problem that felt bigger than my studio.

I could see the work with my eyes and touch it with my hands. I could sketch, cut, shape, polish, stitch, refine, and finish. But the online world did not care that I had talent. It did not care that I had history. It did not care that my work carried a name, a people, a memory, and a meaning.

It only cared about one thing: could the right person find me, trust me, and take the next step with me?

That question is the real reason this book exists.

I have met many skilled people whose work never travels beyond their street, not because their work is weak, but because their message is hidden. I have also met people with average skills who succeed simply because they learned how to show up online with clarity and consistency. That truth can feel unfair, but it is also freeing, because it means the problem is not your destiny. It is your system.

If you read this far, I want you to know something personal.

I did not write this as a "marketing expert" speaking from a high chair. I wrote it as a builder who has felt the fear of posting the first time, the shame of low engagement, the confusion of too many tools, and the pressure of trying to look professional while still learning.

That is why I used stories. That is why I used characters. Nyakor is a guide in the book, but she also stands for something real: the voice that says, "Stop hiding. Start building."

So here is my final message to you.

Do not wait for perfect equipment.
Do not wait for perfect confidence.
Do not wait until you have a hundred products, a flawless website, or a thousand followers.

Start with what you have.

Start with a simple website that tells the truth.
Start with one platform where your people already gather.
Start with one helpful piece of content each week.
Start with one email list that you own.
Start with one repeatable rhythm you can keep.

If you do that, you will not only market. You will build trust.

And trust is the real currency online.

I also want you to remember this: digital marketing is not a personality contest. It is not for loud people only. It is not for "born salespeople." It is for builders who are willing to learn, measure, adjust, and keep going.

Some days you will post and nothing will happen. Do not panic.
Some weeks your reach will fall. Do not quit.
Some people will mock your early work. Do not fight them.
Improve your work and keep moving.

If your message is honest and your system is consistent, growth will come.

Not as a miracle, but as a result.

Before you close this book, I want you to take one action today. Only one.

Choose the action that scares you the least, but moves you forward the most:

- publish your first post

- fix your homepage headline
- write your "About" page as a real story
- create one landing page for your offer
- set up your email list
- write the next blog post title and outline it
- record a short video explaining one thing you know well
- reply to five comments like you mean it
- look at your analytics for ten minutes and write down what is working

One action.

Because the biggest danger is not failure. The biggest danger is delay.

And if you ever feel overwhelmed, come back to this simple truth:

Your work deserves to be found.
Your story deserves to be heard.
Your craft deserves a path.

Build the path. Keep it clear. Keep walking.

Copies, Permissions, and Bulk Orders

If you would like to order copies in bulk for:

- schools and student programs
- churches and discipleship groups
- entrepreneurship clubs
- business trainings and workshops
- staff development for organizations
- gifts for teams, mentors, or graduates

You can request bulk pricing and delivery arrangements through the contacts below.

If you would like to quote short sections of this book, reproduce parts of it, or adapt it for training materials, please request written permission.

Publisher and contact information
Discipleship Press
Web: www.discipleshippress.wordpress.com
Email: maluthabiel@gmail.com
Phone: +254 110 424 822, +211 927 145 394
P.O. Box 28448-00100, Nairobi, Kenya

When writing, include:

- The title of the book: **Digital Marketing Success: Your Digital Presence**
- The format you want (paperback or other)
- The quantity you need
- Your delivery location
- Your preferred timeline
- Whether you want signed copies

If you are an organization and you want training based on this book, include a short note about your group and your goal. I often tailor workshops based on the level of the audience, from beginners building their first website to teams trying to build steady online visibility.

Leave a Review

Reviews are not just for the author. They help other readers decide whether a book is right for them.

If this book helped you, even in a small way, I would be grateful if you left a review where you bought it. A short review is enough.

If you are not sure what to write, here are a few simple prompts:

- What problem were you trying to solve when you started reading, and did this book help you move forward?
- What chapter or idea made you take action, and what action did you take?
- Who would you recommend this book to, and why?

If the book did not meet your expectations, you can still leave an honest review. Honest reviews help me improve and help readers choose better.

Thank you for supporting my work.

About the Author

John Monyjok Maluth writes for builders.

He writes for the person with a gift who feels invisible.

He writes for the person with a message who struggles to package it.

He writes for the person with a business who wants to grow without losing integrity.

John is known by the name **Panyim** in his storytelling voice, a name that carries the weight of memory and origin. In this book, "Panyim" is the narrator and guide, learning in public, applying the lessons, and turning fear into a system.

John's work sits at the meeting point of craft, technology, and meaning. He believes that digital tools are not enemies of tradition. When used with honesty, they are bridges. They help a local maker speak to a global audience. They help a small service compete with larger brands. They help a new writer reach readers without gatekeepers. They help an ordinary person build a path in a noisy online world.

He writes in a direct, practical style, because he has lived in places where time, electricity, and stable internet cannot be assumed. In those conditions, theory is not enough. A person needs steps they can apply, even with limited resources.

In his wider body of work, John writes about growth, discipline, entrepreneurship, identity, and the hard work of building a meaningful life. He also writes about community, dignity, and the responsibility that comes with influence.

He believes that a brand is not a logo first. A brand is a promise. And a promise must be kept.

If you want to connect with John's writing and projects, use the contacts listed in the copyright page and the copies section of this book.

www.ingramcontent.com/pod-product-compliance
Lightning Source LLC
Chambersburg PA
CBHW031416210526
45464CB00005B/1913